A Year in the Life
of a Suburban Allotment

*Or, why a middle-aged, middle-class woman
decided she wanted to grow her own veg.,
finally winning first prize in a pumpkin
competition...*

*One
Woman's
Plot*

One Woman's Plot
Geraldine Kilbride

Five Leaves Publications

One Woman's Plot

Published in 1997 by Five Leaves Publications,
PO Box 81, Nottingham NG5 4ER

Five Leaves Publications
receives financial assistance from:

EAST
MIDLANDS
ARTS

Design by 4 Sheets Design & Print
Printed in Great Britain by Chas. Goater, Nottingham.

ISBN 0 907123 86 4

Chapter 1
In The Beginning Was The Carrot

Proverb
S(he) that is in town in May, loses her spring.

It was the last straw, the clincher, the bridge too far —
the article on pesticides in carrots — and as a struggling
vegetarian, I finally had to take action.

I was a struggling vegetarian, because I kept forgetting
to tell people that I had "gone veggie". This meant that I
just had to poke down that pig or lamb or chicken after my
conscientious hostess had gone to so much trouble — prin-
cipally to include me on the guest list at all, given my leg-
endary unreliability. To come up with a pathetic, "Don't
worry, I'll just eat the vegetables", didn't seem sufficient
recompense for such a display of faith and friendship.

It wasn't merely in the cause of sustaining a social life,
however, that I was engaged in this struggle, I often
drooped under the strain of putting something together of
a vegetarian bent. Rice and... (usually carrots) takes a lot
of putting together — in my book, anyway, though the
Time and Motion pedants will argue the toss *vis-à-vis*
meat and two veg. But roasting and frying were part of my
cultural heritage, they came naturally to me. Chips, egg,
sausage and any other meat, apart from brains (which are
certainly not "meat" as we know it Captain) were all bat-
tered, beaten and baked to a crisp where I came from.

Steaming, sautéing and stir-frying (using a wok ?!) were
customs into which I was painfully initiated after a long

sojourn in the South and then none too adroitly. But I have managed to hold out against micro-waving because of its association, in my mind, with X-rays and Martian fall-out.

It seemed to me that culinary skills divided quite sharply down the middle of the metaphorical plate, which contained meat on the right hand side and veggies on the left. All of the cooking words beginning with "S", those soft, sibilant, strange words, were strongly allied to the culinary world of the veg., whereas my traditions had pre-pared me only for cooking life on the hoof. Hence my slow, my very, very slow conversion to green eating and eating greens.

Proverb:
Nature hates all sudden changes

As you can see, it is not nor never was, that meat held no attraction for me. *Au contraire,* a quick-fix of a couple or three ham sandwiches, oozing cucumber and sweet pickle and hoovered up while watching the racing on the telly on a Saturday afternoon, will ever be a honeyed memory of an undisciplined and rebellious early middle age.

In order to persevere with my intent, though, I continu-ally rehearsed the arguments in favour of my chosen course. Lower cholesterol, a lean and limber body, better use of land resources, less expensive nutrition, increased food variety (hah), dead animals. You've probably guessed which was the clincher.

It was while enjoying one of my ham sandwiches, a thicker, oozier version, using door-step granary bread and Normandy butter, that I watched the programme on pig rearing. Nothing about friendly, pinkish pigs in muddy fields enjoying life in the altogether cute piggy versions of the nissan hut, which you see everywhere these days. Rather, the gross, fat grey variety of pig, chained permanently into a stall, where it eats, breeds, shits and then is hauled away to be slaughtered. I saw that part too.

That was about it for me. I made the decision, then and there, while finishing the sandwiches, naturally, but in the mental mode of the Last Supper. I was going to stop eating meat.

This felt like an important decision, one which would doubtless involve sacrifice and change, but would be for my own "good" and that of the industrialised animal kingdom as a whole. But it was a lot less momentous than deciding to become a vegetarian, because I hadn't. I was quite clear in my own mind that giving up meat was not the same as becoming a vegetarian. Why? Well, it has something to do with the aura attendant on true vegetarians, the kind of people they are and the life they lead — or my perception of them anyway. My life was not going to change, in any way other than at meal times. I was not about to espouse Hindu philosophy, wear tie-dye or drink parsnip wine rather than claret.

That was my clear intention then and I look back on over two years of increasingly more rather than less vegetarian experience and I am frankly bemused by the changes that have occurred in me, in ways that seem largely unconnected with what I eat. Funny how life takes over and pushes you down paths you never intended to take and moulds you in ways you would resist given any conscious choice in the matter!

Anyway, what about this allotment?

I was jogging along eating vegetables. I bought them in greater quantities and attempted to add greater variety in vegetable type. I didn't invest in books about lentils or mung beans and I have always mentally sniggered at the thought of nut cutlets. But I did, eventually, have to investigate how to cook brown rice. My original efforts were absolutely disgusting. The stuff always came out tasting like grit, the equivalent of what you see pigeons eating in Trafalgar Square, but once I had actually read the instructions on the packet, I developed a pride in my finished

3

product. Brown rice became something of a staple; I could put it in the pan, double the quantity of water, turn on the gas and go away and do something else, actually for quite a long time — the only problem then being, what to eat with it.

And it became quite a significant problem. Supermarkets, my favourite mode of shopping, as they are non-interactive, bar basic pleasantries with the check-out person, became less than the huge warehouses of limitless choice that I'd previously experienced them as being. Layer upon layer of shelving, aisle after aisle of produce yet still only your basic two sorts of cabbage, three sorts of lettuce, two of tomatoes and a few swedes, turnips and bags of potatoes thrown in. That was fine for about a month. After that, I began to be seriously bored. I felt disadvantaged as a no meat and two veg. eater. I hunted out those supermarkets offering sweet potatoes and yams as an alternative, with butternut squash and salsify making the odd appearance. But really, I felt that if I had been a dog or cat, I would have been significantly better provided for in terms of choice and variety.

Better luck in the next reincarnation.

But then, even the government began to show signs of strain. I mean, when the government admits, even if only on page 5 of your regular, daily newspaper, tucked below a glamorous car ad., that all may not be well with the basic carrot as it is grown on the carrot-prairies of Lincolnshire — then, I think you might justifiably give up and panic. And I did.

Voilà, the allotment.

I was used to giving my carrots a bit of light work with a brush under the tap. They were my vegetarian equivalent of chips-with-everything. Bursting with beta caratene, I ate carrots in many forms and luxuriated in the certain knowledge that this was health with a capital "H".

Wrong again. Carrots, as we were now warned, were actually bursting with a chemical cocktail sufficient to put one's very life at risk — unless peeled. Apparently, peeling makes everything all right again, though I have still to discover how much you have to peel off before you get back to the "safe" bits and which carrots have to be operated on. Because, to complicate things just that little bit more, of those carrots tested by H.M.G., only 25% revealed these noxious substances. Better odds, by far, of ingesting some life-threatening material, than winning the National Lottery — though that has also proved to be life-threatening on occasion. But I didn't feel cool about throwing away every fourth carrot, peeling the rest to within an inch of their life and woking the remains.

Another remedy was called for and like the clarion call from heaven, it came to me — "Woman, get an allotment".

Proverb
S(he) that follows Nature is never out of her way.
Nature is conquered by obeying her.

I am fortunate enough to live in a borough which believes in allotments. Though a very leafy, well-parked and private-gardened borough by London standards, there are a few pockets of flat-dwellers land, where we, impecunious remnant, live without the benefit of our own gardens.

Stacked on top of each other, but not to the dizzying heights of Central London — usually only three or four stories high at most, we, in this flat-land, have a choice of about 25 sites around and about the area to feed our need for a piece of earth to call our own.

I was not born with this information, you understand, I had come across various allotment sites on walks and bike rides around the area, but had somehow thought of them as being not of my world, but parallel to it.

Serried rows of wig-wamed, cane structures, burgeoning plots of onion rows, their firm, fleshy tops, poking white and naked from the earth and the areas where the owners had obviously given up and left nature to run wild and

5

woolly, had made no serious impression on me. I saw these things, but took no real notice of them, being, as they were for me, just another feature of the landscape. So I had to do some serious research to establish the necessary allotment lore, when I decided that I was going to try and get one.

Again, my borough came to my aid. I presumed that I would have to spend days on the telephone tracking down obscure application forms from diverse departments — left dangling while people made lengthy enquiries of colleagues which would prove fruitless and that absolutely nobody would bother to ring back with information as promised.

But no. My borough produced both a leaflet and a person devoted to this, my cause. Both were helpful, informative, chatty and reassuring. The former was printed in an appropriate green and gave useful hints, warnings and encouragement, generally of a chemical-free nature, to help production using organic methods :-

"Remove caterpillars by hand and try sinking jam jars containing beer in the soil or inverted grapefruit rinds for slug traps."

Obviously, I brushed lightly past this advice. There was certainly no way that I would be moved to come into physical contact with any crawling creature, whether caterpillar or slug, even if shielded by industrial-strength rubber gloves. I would trust to luck to get an allotment that didn't have that kind of legless, slimy problem — or I'd complain and send it back.

What is more, the picture of me filling jam jars rather than myself with beer and scattering discarded grapefruit halves like some kind of gay rite-of-spring ceremonial was utterly absurd. I was indulgent and kind to the writer of this advice and would be equally so, to those who chose to follow it — but oh no, not me babe!

Jacky, Allotments Liaison and Administration Officer, was very open and friendly and did not ask searching questions to establish either my gardening credentials or suitability in general. It was enough that I wanted one. This was a rare experience in itself. I had to prove or demonstrate nothing at all. I did not have to have "previous experience" — a *sine qua non* of the world of applications — nor a long lineage of green-fingered ancestors, nor even a father mentioned in horticultural dispatches.

Jacky did not require that I produce references attesting to good character nor assurances that I could grow anything at all, nor that I would. I felt that to lay down Astroturf, park cars and sell ice-creams would have been acceptable, in this sudden and startling arena of unconditional acceptance.

I had experienced nothing like it before. I wanted something that was on offer and I was being treated, not like someone with something to hide, an adversary who's real motivation (of a dark and disreputable nature) it was her duty to uncover — I was being treated like a real human being, whom Jacky was there to help.

Banks, building societies and other "service" industries should be paying a large consulting fee to the allotment sector to learn about dealing with people — not just customers or worse, consumers — who respond to their expensive advertising, and ask for what's on offer. "I'd like a mortgage please, or can I have a loan please?" The officials in banks *et al* seem to be highly trained in making you feel small and insignificant and somehow guilty for wanting these services — for which, let us not forget, you pay and pay through the nose.

I was told I could even choose my own plot, subject to it not being otherwise engaged. Choice! Again I was taken aback. No allocation, no waiting until something becomes available — nothing pre-determined, pre-arranged and pre-empted by a bureaucracy bigger and heavier than me. I could choose.

That became my next task. I had my eye on an area of allotments, literally over the road from my block of flats. That "road" is the South Circular, which for those unfamiliar with London's routes, practices, along with its brother, the North Circular, in being the M25.

They learned a lot about a London orbital route from these two roads. They learned that people and their habitats, like schools, shops, houses etc., get in the way of the traffic. It has to keep stopping and starting because people, like chickens, just seem drawn to the other side of the road. I don't know what the M25's excuse is though.

This set of allotments, once reached has a great deal of charm. It lies opposite a school and has Beverley Brook bordering one side. I was familiar with the site, as I use that road, as an escape route from the proto-M25, when I'm on my way to pay a call on the deer in Richmond Park. In fact, once across the South Circular, the scenery rapidly becomes stiller, leafier, richly green and altogether more delightful.

Not only can I cycle past the allotments, a fascinating composition of varied design and growth, but I can take a little bridge across the brook and enter the charms of Palewell Common. This large, lush expanse of well-mown meadow comes complete with tennis courts, for which you do not have to book at least a month in advance, as at Clapham Common; a Pitch and Put course and a small tea-shop. This is a real find. It is open all year round and is run by a down-to-earth, thankfully un-middle-class woman, who brings her dog with her. She provides the odd sandwich as well as tea for the adult visitor and crisps and cola for the school kids who have, thoughtfully, provided much in the way of mural decoration all over the outside walls.

With the tea-shop on my right, I can cycle a path which skirts the common and leads directly to the Park gates of Roehampton, where, on hot days I can stop and buy an ice-cream from the van, before cycling on into the huge, regal spaces of Richmond Park and the deer.

Naturally, this would be my first choice, if at all possible.

*

I made an appointment to see Eric, who was in charge of

this site as well as two others, so was apparently keen, not only on gardening, but on administration as well, or on "being in charge".

Chapter 2
Lamb's Lettuce, or Nettles?

Proverb
*If you leap into a well, Providence is not bound
to fetch you out.*

I cycled round to the gates of the allotment and shouted
for Eric, as he had instructed me to, over the phone. The
site was locked, as it always is — you have to have a key to
get in, which you pay a deposit for. This is in the hope of
stopping vandals from stealing things like flowers and vegetables, which others have sweated over for months. Hope-
fully, the key-system also protects the contents of the
sheds, which almost every allotment comes provided with.
In here can be kept tools, canes, wire, compost, any spare
grapefruit halves you might have saved up and the drink.
I was keen on the last element anyway, believing that all
work and no play, was likely to make me very dull indeed.
I only hoped that I would have enough room in my shed for
the sun-lounger and matching parasol job which I had my
eye on.

A fit looking forty-something chap, dressed in black with
close cropped grey hair let me in. I remember registering
positive here, because my prejudices, which usually work
overtime, had me believing that everyone in allotment-
land, would remind me of Colonel Blimp and his wife.

This guy called over to Eric. I just had time to notice
that the Stephen Berkoff look-alike had got things very

smartly organised around his slice of land, when Eric advanced, pen and paper in hand.

Eric was not warm. I noticed this quite quickly and tried to compensate by being nice, girlish and warm enough for the both of us. Eric also had the kind of light blue eyes, in a lightly tanned face that I tend to fall into. Eric was also well past 50 at my reckoning and, in fact, being retired to run allotments, meant that he was probably even older than that. He wore a fetching blue base-ball cap, which had originally seduced me into an easy, but unsuitable familiarity with him. Eric obviously wore his to protect him from the sun alone, and not to signal a funky, laid-back temperament.

Cutting through the "Hello Eric, I spoke to you on the phone, my name is..." chat, like a hot knife through butter, Eric walked me down to the first allotment on offer.

Number 80 was O.K. I picked up Eric's clues very quickly — he evidently didn't think much of it. According to him, it would need a lot "putting back into the ground. It's been mis-used." I wondered, briefly, how you mis-used ground, then checked out the shed accommodation and was surprised to find an almost new child's bike in it.

"Er, it looks like an almost new child's bike has been left in here Eric."

Unconcern. "Yes, well somebody had this site, but as you can see, they've done very little with it. I even helped them to clear it out a bit at first, you know, but they've let it go. We can't have that you know. If people don't keep up their allotments, we can take them back off them." He squared up to me, "If you're not prepared to put at least 3fi hours into the allotment, every week, it's not worth taking on."

Hasty reassurances from me, coupled with increased warmth and niceness. "Oh, I was reckoning to spend more time than that Eric. I work from home, you know, so it should be easy for me." I felt that I was given a look.

As we strolled up the path to No 64 I chewed over my rash promise. Work from home though I did, time just

11

slipped by so easily and frighteningly. What with actually working, which I seemed to do precious little of, washing, cleaning, ironing, not to mention the desirables such as yoga, shopping, horse-riding, bike-riding etc. etc. to say nothing of art galleries, museums, the theatre and the cinema — all had to be fitted in (paying for it all was another matter), in order that my life be full, and rich and rounded. This was the very reason why I wasn't hounding the recruitment agencies and scouring the classified ads to find another 9 to 5 job. At my age, I wanted more of something different, something more relaxed and subtle, something that people seemed to call "quality of life", even if I couldn't afford it.

How had I managed to fit in any of that other stuff before, when I was an ambitious careerist — in the lunch hour? Week-ends?

So just when did I think I was going to do my allotment? I pushed these uncomfortable thoughts aside as we came up to No 64. It came as a surprise to me, because it was hidden from the road and screened, at its rear, by houses and their gardens. It felt quiet and secluded, more rural, less industrial. It was also shockingly large and head-high in weeds.

Eric waxed enthusiastic. Good ground, easy to clear, "Just scythe down the growth, stack it to dry, then burn it." What, I thought, burning in a pollution-free zone?

"Carefully though, so as not to disturb others", he breezily countered my unspoken objections. "Then spread weed-killer all over it and it'll be ready to work in a matter of weeks."

This time, he must have heard my intake of breath. Gardening novice though by now he knew I was, I was already firmly anti-pesticides and sprays. This was the whole *raison d'etre* of taking on an allotment, to get away from eating food that contained most of ICI's finest.

Eric, though, was firm on this one. "I've been an horticulturalist all my life and as a professional, I know the value of things like weed-killer. People who go on about organic methods, don't know what they're talking about. How do you think we manage to feed people in this country? How do we manage to produce all these surpluses? Fertilisers work, that's why we use them."

I gazed at him during this outburst, my limited gardening-brain, though reeling under the attack from somebody who knew something about gardening, felt like biting back about the uselessness of all these surpluses — grain and butter mountains, and wine lakes and the Common Agricultural Policy. The pity was though, that despite being familiar with the headings, I didn't really know anything about the issues, just that they were there and we had them. I was certainly in no position of fact sufficient to argue any corner. Besides, Eric was the one in control here, if I launched into a half-baked defence of chemical-free growing methods, he may have taken the promise of my piece of God's own land away from me — and by now, I really, really wanted one.

Not necessarily this one, however. Bigger than the allotments round and about it, 6 rods, as I later found out. (I know, bear with me, learning new things keeps you young. 5 rods is equal to 30ft by 45ft, and this one was bigger). In another life it could have been a natural habitat for orangutangs, complete with odd pieces of metal structure, looking like it was left over from an ape-friendly climbing frame assemblage you see in zoos. I gazed down its length and tried to imagine neatness, order and disciplined growth. I couldn't.

But Eric was pumping enthusiasm into me. Of course, I later learned from a fellow allotmenter that No 64 was regularly offered to new recruits and equally regularly rejected by people with more sense and less need to please. I, however, was swayed by location. It was a quieter, pleasanter patch of ground and I could lose myself in its far distance, unobserved by more experienced eyes. And, as the estate agents tell us, location is everything.

Sensing that I was almost sold, Eric relented, a bit, and I, feeling that I had done the right thing, or was going to, stretched the boundaries of exchange and asked to see his plot.

Of course, Eric was the possessor of not just one plot, but two. On learning, however, that he had to take two bus rides to get from his home in Fulham to the site, I guessed that having only the one plot would hardly make the journey worthwhile. Blushing at my own lack of commitment in wanting a site, which I could virtually water from my balcony and which would probably take me a full five minutes slow walk to get to, I followed Eric to his first patch, expecting to be dazzled.

Frankly, I wasn't. There were no four foot beds, surrounded by planks of wood and neat paths; no raised beds of mixed growth of feathery green and marigolds, which my reading had led me to suspect were *de rigeur* in the fight against carrot fly. There were some irises. I struggled to find something appropriate to say. There were also a couple of rows of something else.

"Oh, what are those? Are they lamb's lettuce?" I felt pleased with my knowledge and relieved to find a healthy row of some veg. that I recognised.

"No, they're nettles. Don't you eat them?" I looked at him.

"I thought everyone ate them. Very good for you, they are."

I gave up. All I wanted was to get out of there. I felt that I'd come to the end of my attempts at relationship with Eric for one day.

We finished the business angle quickly. He'd send off my forms to Jacky. She'd send back some forms to me; I'd pay some money and then, Bob's your uncle — time to arrange the allotment-clearing party.

Chapter 3
The Tools of the Trade

Chinese Proverb
With patience the mulberry leaf becomes a silk gown.

It is in the garden of patience that strength grows best.

Well, apparently all I had to do then was wait and I did, for two weeks, which came as a disappointment after the casual speed with which things had been accomplished up till then.

Of course, the weather, in late June, after being absolutely foul, chose to display exceptionally fine atmospheric conditions for life in general, though perhaps not so for gardeners come to think of it — ie. it was hot and dry. A friend of mine, who was rather encouraging about the whole procedure, obviously wanting a bit of a share for her and her kids, began to get fretful about the delay.

"We (note the "we") need to get a few things in before the end of June so that we don't miss this season entirely." I agreed with her for good form's sake, but given the amount of digging and clearing that was obviously required, I doubted that we'd be doing much planting anyway, but lots more of the non-creative stuff including laying down well-rotted horse-manure and/or a green compost like comfrey — which my friend had in her garden.

We had a source for the horse-manure too, in the four

stables that sit on the corners of Richmond Park and once we got going, we'd be sure to build ourselves a decent compost heap.

I enjoyed all those details. I had got some guides to growing vegetables from the local primary school's summer fair, very cheaply, and I would sit and decide what I was going to grow. I was a bit confused as to when you put things in to match their growing season, and the abundance of varieties available made me a bit nervous in case I went for the "wrong" type.

In fact, given all the factors that you have to take into account, type of soil, PH factor (yes, just like your skin), sun or shade, early, middle or late cropping as well as what kind of bugs and disease one's plot was prey to — the selection process felt as complicated as a game of 3 dimensional chess (probably feels). Perhaps there is a software programme which can take account of all these factors and produce the perfect variety for all conditions, resulting in perfect plants for beginners.

In the end I decided to relax and let trial and error teach me best practice along with helpful hints from allotment *confrères* — and my friend.

I then moved on to pricing useful items at the local DIY superstore. I was on safer ground here, shopping comes naturally to most people, I think, and I could pass exams in How to Make a Purchase. I drifted around shelves of items like wheel-barrows and hoses which appeared to be shockingly expensive, as well as more arcane gadgets like compost bins which come complete with worms to aid the tilth. These animals are called Tiger worms, probably due to the aggressiveness with which they attack your old boiled egg shells and cabbage leaves. I was amazed that I'd so far got through life without knowing that you could buy a specialised worm to eat your natural rubbish and spew it out as high grade, garden compost. You can even get these bins and worms by post from the seed catalogues, which left me wondering just how well the worms would travel by Royal Mail.

I had the very basic tools already, spade, fork, rake so given the estimated cost of the additional tools, I decided to re-direct my search to junk shops and thrift shops and just generally to ask around to see if anyone had a spare barrow or 200 foot hose.

One nearly always has more than one of these items left over from Christmas and weddings, I find.

I did go and have another look at my intended allotment, one Sunday morning. I wanted to get to know it at different times of day and even different days because, like most properties, I believed its character would change not merely seasonally, but with each angle of the sun and drift of cloud.

It was busy. People were coming and going as frequently as at Sainsbury's, which was new. Previously, I'd seen the area only dotted with the occasional bowed figure, quietly weeding, watering or gathering. Now the place hummed. The reason for all this activity was that the shop was open. The shop, open for about an hour, either Saturday or Sunday mornings, was the place to buy mushroom compost, canes and ... all at reasonable prices. It was staffed by "volunteers" — allotmenters roped in by Eric, to do their service, their bit for the wider allotment community. It seemed a lively place, people were chatting and trundling around with carts piled with the bagged compost and heavily engaged in yet more chatting.

People chatted to me too. Never having seen me before, I imagined that the regulars' response to me would be the same as going to a new club or church — neutral glances, but no actual approach. Here, it was wildly different. I was hailed by "hellos" from all sides as I walked down to No 64. People were open and curious, in the nicest way. Soon, I was giving anyone the story-so-far and receiving lots of good lucks and good wishes. I could tell, however, that they thought No 64 a) required a lot of work and b) that it was too big. Of course, I was well aware of these obstacles, but somehow, seeing them reflected in others, only made me more nervous on the inside and more bluff, "Oh, I'm sure I'll manage," on the outside.

I got to meet my neighbour to the right, also an Eric. He seemed to be a very gentle man, who had had his allotment for 18 years. He was nice enough to hope that I got the allotment and to feed me words of encouragement,

"You've got to take it gently. Don't worry about not doing everything at once. That's not what it's about. You've got to enjoy it. I love my allotment, though I've not been too well recently and things have got out of hand a bit. But still, it doesn't matter. The best thing is to try and keep the weeds down."

"Eric, The Boss," the future and forever distinction between the Erics, "...says that I should put weed-killer on it, but I don't feel comfortable about that". I said anxiously, knowing, intuitively, that Eric, The Neighbour, would agree with me.

"Me, neither," he said. "It stays in the ground such a long time, but I know that's what he thinks."

We smiled at each other.

"I hope you enjoy your allotment and get a lot of pleasure out of it." I thanked him and walked on up the path towards the secret door which leads out onto the South Circular and across to my block of flats.

I never saw him again.

Shortly after this meeting, though I went down to the allotment to continue the Clearance, most evenings, Eric was not about. I went away for a two week holiday in the last weeks of July and I came back to learn that he had died. His struggle with cancer had ended.

I went to his funeral because, though having only met him the once, he had made a strong impression on me for the good. The church was not full, though I spotted a couple of other people from the allotment who had also come to pay their respects.

Allotments are like that, I think, they breed cama-raderie. Some people have their allotments for years and the friendships that develop are often quiet but mature.

For myself, even that first Sunday, I felt as though I had been accepted and made to feel welcome — more easily and naturally than I had experienced almost anywhere else. Perhaps it's all part of being close to the ground and taking part in making things grow, it brings people back to basics.

That morning, allotmenters were behaving as though it was the norm to accept others, to include them, rather than to be withdrawn until a sufficient amount of time elapsed to remove the "stranger" label. It was a more unfeigned and automatic response than that practiced by official welcome groups I'd recently experienced such as at church or the Residents Association of the flats I lived in. Yet, surprisingly, people belonging to both church and association were also allotmenters — I had met and said hello to one or two people from each and found it far eas-ier to talk to them at the site than at either church or my flats. The fact of having an allotment brought us together in a unique way.

Early days, I reminded myself. It could still all end in tears.

Chapter 4
Early July

Proverb
Where the cause is, there shall be the eagles gathered together.

My friend got rather agitated at the delay in receiving the keys to the allotment and after daily phone calls to me for a week to see if they had arrived, she took matters in hand and called Jacky.

Needless to say, the delay was my fault. I had not seen nor read on the form that I was meant to send in £10 deposit for said keys. Without my friend's intervention, we could have been hanging around for weeks without getting our hands dirty!

We discussed when we would get together and launch our endeavour. By now it had become "our" project. There was too much allotment for one person, and besides, I already knew that I needed lots of help and encouragement, particularly when the novelty inevitably wore off and my friend was ideal for supplying both.

The "launch" was planned around a bottle of some kind and a few sympathetic friends, well chosen for their general empathy for gardens and gardening and the likelihood that they would participate in the grand clearing.

The said day arrived, in mid-week to avoid the crowds Jane and Seamus, plus their dog, duly turned up at lunchtime. I was rather disappointed to note that Jane was got up in Henley gear rather than "down on the farm" kit and made it clear that she was not in the mood for manual labour. She felt more drawn to the celebration element of the proposed event and even that was pushing it — I could tell that the thought of an "allotment" struck her as a mite too plebeian and not her idea of a good time. Seamus, on the other hand, looked entirely the thing; tall, broad, Irish and in jeans and stout boots.

My friend, plus one of her children off sick from school, appeared fortuitously as I was about to get antsy with Jane about her lack of sense of occasion. Instead, we sat down to picnic on my living-room floor so as to gird the loins with sustenance, enhance the mood and relax everyone before we got "down and dirty" to the allotment and the real business of the day.

All too soon, there were just no more egg sandwiches left and while the sun was still high in the sky, we moved across the road to libate the plot with a bottle of fizz thoughtfully provided for the occasion by my friend.

Seamus, and even Jane, fell for the site as soon as we had shut the wooden gate behind us and were in the depths of allotment land. Every patch or plot had its own character and charm and something to admire in the plant line, and we all got rather high on the sights and smells and the prospect of growing things.

Jane and I walked up and down the paths, plastic cups in hand, waxing lyrical about nature and good husbandry, while my friend and Seamus explored our site and found vegetation we could keep among the nettles and couch grass and bindweed.

A herb that we couldn't ignore among our weeds was the curry plant. There was quite a distinctive patch of it — grey, filigree foliage topped with yellow flowers, but its demure aspect and modest size was as nothing compared to its smell. A strong waft of tandoori hit you as you came up the path to our plot and got stronger and more vindalooish the nearer you dared come to its source. In the same area were also fennel, thyme and mint, all vigorous and pungent, vying with each other for scents sensation, but all hopelessly eclipsed by the good, spicy, pungent curry aroma. Like the food, you either love or loathe it, but it wont be ignored.

Although allotments, by their very proximity, tend to "share" species which drift and self-seed, I noticed that no other allotment had such a showing of curry plant — due, no doubt, to vigorous censorship by their owners. This was just as well, really, as otherwise, on a warm day, working on the allotment would have felt and smelt similar to working in a Bombay restaurant.

We found other items on the site such as endless plastic bin-bags, bits of wooden stakes and bamboo canes, glass panes and netting — a hotchpotch of gardening memorabilia, revealing evidence of earlier serious growing intent. We also found a lot of blackberry bushes which I, in my ignorance, was quite pleased about — free fruit, I thought, and no more organised walks, foraging for the stuff along country lanes armed with indiscreet buckets and (complaining) small children.

An allotment associate, however, warned me, not very many days later, that the ubiquitous blackberry should actually be regarded more as a weed because it propagates itself all over the show and has great big, sterling, spreading roots which you can never entirely dig up. As, by this time, on those same bushes, I had scratched my legs so often that the marks resembled red netting, I was vowing vengeance and destruction on them anyway and was glad to have my baleful intentions justified.

The other major item we found on our patch was a wasps' nest in the compost heap. I could have cared less about this, frankly, until I discovered that the wasps had also taken up squatters' rights in our tool shed.

The tool shed already suffered from being festooned inside and out, but mostly inside, by a creeping vine which seemed to prefer it in there to the outside; so, what with the creeper and the wasps, the shed was not going to see much active service.

Too keen to worry about these niggles on the day, however, we felt that our predecessors had probably been more or less organic as we were relieved to find no empty slug-pellet canisters nor weed-killer containers. Our eventual produces would, so we swore, be more rather than less free of chemicals — unless we gave up along the way and decided to spray for Britain to ensure some veg. from the plot.

Though Seamus got right down to it and started pulling up long bundles of yellowish grass, the rest of us were too drunk with wine and excitement to do anything sensible.

My friend had, though, got the loan of a hand-scythe. She had wrapped the working end of this grim-reaper prop in plastic bags but had still got stern and mistrustful looks from the driver and puzzled looks from fellow passengers as she struggled to load herself, plus child, plus implement onto the bus for the journey. The scythe stood over six feet tall and was in no way a discreet object. On a small Hopper bus filled with ladies and the elderly, all bundled with shopping bags after a trip to the supermarket, my friend must have looked a cut above your usual bag lady.

Anyway, since she had bothered to lug this thing down to the plot, we decided to have a go. For about ten minutes I watched my friend as she heaved through the undergrowth, hoping for a Thomas Hardy effect of smooth, swinging strokes, glistening muscles and defeated plant life. Obviously this wasn't what we got and so I decided that I should have a go. The problem lay in the greenery itself. It resisted. Corn and wheat, having been specially bred and trained to do so, might once have fallen to the blade in "Tess of the D'Urbevilles", but our growth wasn't having any of it.

Rather than successfully cutting the growth back to an earthly crew-cut, we generally only managed to bend it — a bit. To my inebriated eyes, it was trying to fool us into believing that we'd defeated it; lying doggo with one large green eye open and upon us, waiting until we'd gone home, before springing back up, proud, strong and a complete nuisance.

This meant all out war.

It also meant that we'd had enough for one day and we decided to execute a tactical withdrawal, laying plans to come back soon, better armed and equipped to wring a submission from the stubborn earth.

We were all exhausted and over-excited by this new toy of ours. My friend and I eagerly agreed to meet the next day to continue the good fight and Seamus and Jane thought that they would come too, and that after Jane's initial coolness. Jane had now, however, decided that she must have an allotment too which I thought was fairly typical. But, for both of them to come the next day would mean that Seamus would have to take more time off work (he had a septic finger) and though strongly wanting the use of Seamus' muscles, gardening skill and general good will and helpfulness, my friend and I earnestly discouraged this idea.

I think that we were almost greedy to be alone with the allotment — to be able to get to know it on our own and plan how we were going to clear it and what we were going to get in the ground as soon as possible; to decide on what bits we would leave in place, like the elderflower and blackberries, or whether they had to be moved or go for good to make way for new plants.

We also wanted to continue the discoveries; we had found rhubarb and raspberries and something great, green and bushy which we felt could have been horse radish.

There was so much to do and in so little time, literally, as we were now into July and without some serious effort on our part, we could be looking at next Spring for any real eatable crop.

Chapter 5
The Real Work Begins.

Chinese Proverb
Every task is easy to a resolute man.

It was not easy clearing our allotment. We never expected that it would be, but the reality still came as a shock. We managed to scythe down the bulk of the weeds to ground level and were left with several piles of "soon to be" compost, blackberry brambles and the elder and a largeish number of blisters, leg scratches and nettle stings. We then got digging.

We began on the north eastern part of the plot, at the back and as far as possible away from the central path and people. There was no great strategic reason for starting there apart from wanting to be away from curious eyes, so that we couldn't be spied on as we forced our way through the sods, which is how we generally referred to each huge, twisting tap root.

We had the compensation, though, of turning up lots of potatoes from this section, to our vast delight — more free food. These we boldly boiled and ate, though we didn't know how long they'd been left in the ground and if they were still good to eat. I actually waited until my friend's boy had eaten about 2lb of them before I had a go — just in case.

The ground, though deeply grassed, was not too heavy to turn over, probably because of having been relatively recently planted up with the potatoes and so we did about half way and then, earnestly covered our dig with black, plastic bin bags to prevent the weeds from springing back, with joy, into this newly clean space.

We'd read about this technique from one of our books on organic gardening. We'd learned that we could use a "ground cover", ideally of carpet, to teach the stubborn weeds a thing or two, but we only had the Number Two Alternative — black plastic bags, of which there were loads just lying around on the plot. Obviously its former owners had been heavily into the punk era and then, at a stroke, abandoned that style for naturism, running off, wantonly, across the allotments, shedding bin bags like rose petals as they fled.

The principle upon which this procedure was said to work, was similar to that of confining prisoners to the black, unlit depths of ancient dungeons, so weeds thus covered, would gradually despair of ever again receiving any light, air or sustenance and so just fade away and die. Some weeds had obviously studied history; others hadn't.

I booked a few dates with other friends, who had, in their middle-class way, expressed admiration, even envy when I revealed the fact of my having an allotment — and had lavished offers of help. I generally see my friends at social events, arranged by others and involving alcohol by the bottle, not the glass, which may have impacted on the eventual offer-to-dig ratio.

One of those offers (and one only), materialised in the form of Sally (ex of the music biz, now of the film biz) who came down from work one evening, to dig.

Sal arrived, in what I admiringly thought were her digging clothes; obviously her commitment and motivation for the task were at an executively high level. As it turned out, her orange shorts and trainers were the stuff of deal-making, power dressing for the really cool — a thousand years away from the hackneyed images seen in the womens' magazines and were not to be confused with the beige shorts and trainers I had on. Convenience dressing for the downwardly mobile.

At the lotty, Sal got down to it, made the right noises about the spiritual value and/or emotional satisfaction of growing your own vegetables or something and did dig. I undermined the whole affair by feeling too embarrassed at imposing hard manual labour on a friend and so ended up by calling time very early. We then repaired to my flat to eat and drink — old habits die hard.

Boredom with this gross, heavy work began to creep in after only about ten days of clearing. In my friend's case, it fairly galloped in, leading reinforcements because, as she said, she had so many seedlings, brought on in her greenhouse at home, which desperately needed to be planted out. We had cleared a patch, so why didn't we just get on with it?

When I arrived a couple of days later to find a small, neat bed prepared of about 8ft by the recommended 4ft, laid out with three rows of green, young plants looking like three kinds of lettuce, my heart swelled. To complement this, my friend had also prepared a shorter bed, of about 5ft by 3ft, into which she had placed 7 tomato plants. To the rear of each of these, she had buried a 4", plastic flower pot, which I at first thought was to catch slugs (in place of the grapefruit halves, remember?). But no, they were to act as water reservoirs and serve two really useful purposes, allowing lots of water to go directly to the root area of the tomato plant, which are greedy for water to swell their fruits and yet they help avoid over-wetting the plant stem, which can cause it damage.

I then rushed out and bought four courgette plants, two aubergines and six pots of sweet corn, these being the only vegetable plants that my local garden centre stocked. I was completely ignorant about the planting conditions and care required by any of these plants. I didn't even like eating aubergine very much except in the ubiquitous moussaka which I had given up because it traditionally contains meat and is hugely fattening. My blood was hot, however, and I wanted to get planting particularly given that my friend had, so far, supplied all the raw material and I had to keep my end up as it were.

Hurrying to my handy guide, which I grabbed to take to the allotment with me in the expectation of illuminating my first planting, I learned that for the courgettes and the corn, I needed to plant into holes filled with peat or compost. This was OK, I could manage the compost, though I worried about the peat given the fast disappearance of peat bogs in Ireland. The aubergine only needed "well cultivated soil".

For a completely amateur, novice gardener such as me, instructions like the above are about as helpful as "add a pinch of salt" or "fold lightly into the mixture" are to the clumsy cook.

Well, what is, well cultivated soil? I was stumped and reduced to the exercise of logic. Obviously, my allotment couldn't be in this "well" class anyway, as, by very definition, no cultivation had yet been done on it at all — well or ill. The best that I could hope for, was that the previous tenant had well cultivated those potatoes we had eaten and I, and my juvenile plants, could get by on that.

In they went, compost into holes first, as required and careful about the spacing, which I overdid for the aubergines, leaving about 2ft between each plant, rather than a recommended 18". After growing a fraction, they looked a bit lost, shrunk into their own vast space with no (aptly named) companion planting for company.

The corn was a great triumph, as I had read about them needing to be planted in a block, not a single, straight row. This helps the wind to help the male bits to pollinate the female cob-forming bits and hence to produce... cobs.

I still feel slightly ridiculous to be taking account of sexuality in plants. This is a hangover from O'Level Biology; I understood that flowers and things needed to reproduce, but it seemed to me that the intervention of sex in this process should be left to the furry end of creation and above. Sensible plants just double up on their corms or rhizomes and get on with it. The thought of plants apeing the pursuit and penetration practiced by fauna-with-legs, just seems silly to me.

I felt justified, after this effort, in going on holiday during a really hot end of July, leaving the responsibility for watering and maintaining the new planting to my friend.

I half-heartedly hoped that I would come back to see that she had finished most of the digging too — though that would be pushing my luck.

Just before I left, however, we were offered another allotment by Liam, who knew my friend from church, and who was leaving London to take up a new life and garden in Sussex. His plot was perfection in terms of the bed system, each bed 4ft by 15ft, neatly surrounded by wooden planks and containing either chunky, healthy growth or a weed free area ready for its next sowing.

My immediate reaction was to abandon No 64 and move, bag and baggage to the well-ordered, no-clearing-required spaces of No 70.

I fairly salivated at the prospect. My friend, however, wanted to have both of them. This brought me up with a start. We were having trouble getting No 64 going properly. Not trouble exactly, but it was obviously not the work of one week-end to clear the ground, dig in organic matter (means well-rotted compost, manure that kind of thing), find enough planks of wood, from skips and dismantled saunas, to put round beds which would be 15ft or so wide, followed, as the final act, by the seed sowing. With Liam's offer, we could cut to the chase and get the seeds down, after a little judicious activity with the rake to get that soil to a "fine tilth".

We talked it over. My view, in favour of an easier life, did not prevail. My friend liked No 64 and as No 70 was on the "other" side, she felt that we should give both a go for a while and discover the pros and cons of each, then if it all got too much (and I was fairly certain it would), we could decide which one to give up, based on our intimate knowledge. I thought she'd gone lotty loopy. I caved in though, because her reasoning seemed to make some sense at the time and I didn't want to spoil our harmonious relations with a fight quite so early in this rustic relationship.

I checked with E.T.B. (Eric, The Boss) and he was most obliging, "....that's fine. What we want on the allotments are keen, enthusiastic people... the office knows about it, they'll be getting in touch with the forms."

I was inordinately pleased at being judged keen and enthusiastic and at being granted such a fine allotment, over what, according to Liam, would have been some stiff competition.

And off I skipped to allotment-free Istanbul.

Chapter 6
August

Proverb
The difficult is done at once; the impossible takes a little longer.

When I returned from my holiday at the beginning of August, I learned that the weather had been hot and sultry in England too, producing the flip-side of the usual complaints about the weather. Now, as a gardener, the hot weather could only mean one thing — watering duty.

I went round to the allotment the day after my return and was stunned to see a 6ft line of wig-wams supporting young runner beans as well as two lines of neat, grass sods acting as pathways in between beds. I also found six Kale plants and four capsicum plants settling in. My friend had been at it again. The area now cleared on No 64 was about 8 sq ft and rather than leave things 'til next Spring before planting because, after all, Nature abhors a vacuum and will sow her own thing if given the opportunity — meaning more weeds, my friend had feverishly stuck in more plants.

My job was to keep them alive, while my friend had her turn at a holiday, a tough call during this extraordinarily hot weather.

My intuition was spot on, this proved to be no mean feat.

The water tank nearest our lotty was about 4 yds from

the bottom of our plot, but then, there was the 45 ft walk to the top of the plot, where the plants grew. The path up the side of the allotment provided its own test of commitment because its entire length was liberally strewn with things which clawed and scratched, reducing my arms and legs to a mesh of thin red lines and big, plastic looking blisters which came up due to heaven knows what. Carrying two loaded buckets that distance, frequently, soon brought on the major horse-sweats and what made it worse was these two buckets of water seemed to go nowhere over our 8 sq ft. Our plants were horribly thirsty under the mediterranean conditions. I started to feel resentful about giving up every evening between 5:30pm and 7pm to weed (by hand) and water. I wondered if the plants we had were outrageous in their demand for drinks because I rarely spotted anyone else lugging water each evening as I did.

Life seemed to be subsumed into these two activities with little time or energy for anything else. Cinema and theatre dropped off the horizon completely and social events had to be arranged around the plant routine, so much so that I started to give drinks and even barbeques on the allotment in return for watering duty. There was even very little time for other lotty tasks; we still had most of the digging and clearing to do on No 64, but it was too hot and the ground was too hard, to make that a viable option. What was worse, there was now No 70 to start planting-up with winter peas, cabbage and anything else in the seed catalogue which said "sow now".

My anxiety was increased as the kale and lettuce were looking decidedly eaten and not by me. I fumed and raged inwardly at this evidence of mal-practice by some sort of enemy species. What I wanted from gardening were the fruits, whether fruity or veggy. I did not want the intervening obstacles to achievement. Between the sowing and the harvesting of plump, ripe, tasty things to eat, I was aiming for a hassle-free ride. At the moment the balance of effort was tipped in my favour and that of tangible reward, skewed heavily towards something alive but probably slimy and disgusting. I thought of slugs. Not that I had seen any, but then, I wasn't really looking out for them. I loathe slugs and snails with a passion that some people reserve for spiders. I considered slug pellets, but felt that succumbing to such a remedy was to abandon organic principles at the first fence.

Luckily, Liam came to my rescue. He said that it was probably pigeons that were eating all the young, juicy growth and that a barrier of netting would be enough to let the plants recover. He even had a stock of old, white nylon net to hand, with which I hastened to cover all the vulnerable varieties. I must say that I thought this was a much better use of the dreaded net curtaining. I had a load of it, squashed into the back of my airing cupboard and was, for once, delighted that I hadn't thrown it away. I went net mad on the allotment. Feeling like a gardening grown-up in using this organic, "barrier method", I covered the newly planted pea and fennel seeds, to stop the birds gorging themselves and ran around covering anything else which showed signs of being chewed. Liam's allotment soon resembled a patch of Indian washing laid out in the sun to dry.

The other satisfying event which occured during this period of drought was that Seamus came and casually set fire to a good third of No 64 and burnt down the weeds and some of the many brambles. It wasn't meant to be like that, of course, he and Jane had ostensibly come, one afternoon, to do a little light watering work (which is how I had described it to them over the phone) and have tea on the allotment.

We had the tea and Jane and I got down to cutting back the brambles, while Seamus started on the long, long watering trek. Jane and I did a tiny bit of it, but we began to sympathise with the feelings of East African village women, minus the pots-on-heads, and eventually left it all to Seamus.

Once that was over, Seamus said that he would burn down the huge heap of waste that had already been accumulated from the Clearance. It went off with a whoosh like a rocket, great sheets of flame shooting out from all sides, enough smoke to make the neighbouring houses complain and terrified the life out of me.

As nothing dreadful happened however and it seemed that Seamus, with the judicious use of a damping-off technique, had everything under control, he spread the fire over another third of the allotment and hence got rid of at least another week's hard weed-pulling.

This left No 64 looking a bit like a moonscape and a lot less like a lush rain-forest, but, what the hell I thought, at least it was going to result in a lot less work. I was fully expecting some retribution, though, and supposed it would most likely come in the form of E.T.B., writing to me, to spell out the dangers of lighting fires in such dry conditions, the polluting consequences of bombfires and threatening penalty points on the allotment lease.

Nothing of the sort happened. A few allotment colleagues even complimented me on the change and said that I should have burnt it all back earlier.

Nevertheless, as a reaction to the trauma of constant watering duty, I began to suffer from hose envy in a big way. The treck with the watering buckets (we weren't even sophisticated enough to have acquired a proper watering can) was a serious disincentive to actually getting our poor, limited veg. their necessary drink in this, the hottest summer for twenty years or for two hundred years or ever since the world began. The reports increased in grim factor every time I watched a weather person, of whom recently there seemed to be a bewildering variety. I could recall the time when there was only John Ketley and a Co of about two others — including the indecipherable one, who should retire and let Rory Bremner take over. Now, however, there was an array of bright suits, shiny hair and a bright green map of Britain in the background, showing none of the usual grey belt, denoting rain. We had become, meteorologically, on a par with Spain.

I watched others hose their allotments unrestrainedly.

Hose bans seemed a matter of no concern to this fraternity, probably because the water came "free" as a council amenity. So, while the borough's lawns shrivelled to a brown dearth, the allotments bloomed, thrived and grew on apace, revelling in the hot sun and copious amounts of water.

Now and again, I would be taken aback by catching sight of a man clutching his hose at pelvic height, a stream of water arching out from between his hands, reminiscent of other functions. But I got used to it and ceased to look twice.

It was through hose-envy that I got to know Bernadette. I had noticed this small, pixie-like figure on several occasions. She has the allotment across the path from mine which she has cultivated with flowers, drift wood, old stones and bricks from skips and a pond which breeds excellent frogs. The whole effect sways between reflecting the abundance of a cottage garden and the bare tranquillity of a Japanese one. It is certainly a long way from the utilitarian, Grow for Victory model of its neighbours and it suits the look of her — small, slender, short bright dyed blonde hair and lobes full of silver earings.

One late afternoon I came to water and to sow some of the seeds which were due in, between July and October. I had peas, fennel, kohlrabi (the purple kind), broad beans, cabbage, a long, white radish and lamb's lettuce. More than enough given that most of No 64 remained undug, but the plan was to plant some in No 70, Liam's well-tilled and vacant beds and as for the rest, I was intending to wet a large section of the burnt ground and dig it over.

I had noticed earlier that me and the neat, petite blond woman were the only people around at that time. She was hosing at the far end of her allotment and we waved to each other.

Despite the tremendous number of allotments, it was rare to see more than about 6 individuals, whatever time of day, busy on their patch. As the area was so quiet, I tended to leave by 8pm at the latest, as I was too well aware of being alone and kept my eyes and ears out on stalks — ready for anything in the way of intruder, which London could throw at me. I was glad, that this time, there was another woman about.

I got down to my job. Wetting the ground with the water buckets, however, soon proved to be a jolly fruitless and irritating task, not suited to my personality type. I gave up and dragged my gear down to No 70.

After considerable effort with the rake over an area which had previously fed and housed a mystery veg., I managed to sow a bed of peas, sparingly as the packet dictated, in their regulation 6" trenches — and was knackered. My back ached and the wasps and flies seemed to be particularly attracted to the vicious-looking bunch of blisters on my leg. I had imagined that seed sowing was one of the lighter allotment billets; but what with the watering disappointments and now this, my grit quotient was being tested to the uttermost and I decided that I had only two ultimate choices. Give it all up, now, before more money was spent and I contracted something really serious from the strange, flying insects and poisonous undergrowth or soldier on, looking forward to the days of home produce and labour devoted to maintenance rather than rock-breaking.

Careful thought resulted in me deciding to think about it tomorrow — so I went back to No 64, where the two, old rusty red chairs were parked, to have my flask of tea and a banana. It was then that it hit me, Blondie was still hosing down her flowers.

What with one thing and another she must have been sloshing water over her allotment for at least an hour, if not longer, which struck me as profligate in this age of threatened stand pipes. I realised now why her neighbour had been trailing himself and his watering can up and down, up and down the path, like a rat in a run, to the watering hole at some distance from his plot — maybe he was fearful that there would be no water left in their mutual tank, or maybe it was a silent, visual protest and he was hoping to bring her to repent of her extravagant water play.

Tough if he did, because Bernie was cool, even lofty about her right to spray. We got talking. It appeared that she was married to the gorgeous Guy who had a wholly practical allotment a few plots down from her — so together, they had achieved an ideal blend of the pragmatic and the fanciful, exhibiting their very selves in the cultivation of their individual patches.

Bernie grows as a form of therapy; it soothes her to occasion colour and form in living things and she is as loving and protective of her plants as others are of children. Her work is unplanned, but looks right and "works" in a way the design gurus strive to achieve, using expensive artefacts which they distress (not half) or carefully place to conjure an artlessly throw-away look in a completely self-conscious fashion.

"Heard you had a party on your allotment the other night", she said. I was caught on the run. I might have made some casual, fun comment about her use of all that water, but she got me first about the party.

"Well, it was hardly a party", I parried, "a few friends came round to help dig and we ended up having a barbeque and a couple of bottles of wine."

"Sounds nice. What time did you leave?" I wondered if I had now been well and truly caught by the allotment police. Barbies and alchohol on the allotments of Richmond Borough. Not the sort of behaviour the council was trying to foster in providing these splendid amenities. Gardeners should be quiet, reflective people, slow of thought and speech and not given to yahoo behaviour; drinking, music and what goes with them should remain in the confines of the leisure centres .... "Er, about 9 or 9:30", I said, "we didn't want to stay too late. Er, I hope we didn't bother anybody." As I said it, I felt like a wuss. I had fallen into a pathetic attempt at toadying to somebody who was almost certainly not in authority, (the blasting with the hose was proof enough of that, if only I had thought about it). I was getting worse.

"Course not. None of their business anyway. Sounds as though you had a nice time."

I relaxed. I got to thinking that in a mild, innocuous way, we were obviously alike; we stood together against the reactionaries who would deny her flowers their water and me, my harmless fun. Our other mutual characteristic was that we at least looked about 10 years younger than the mean age of allotment-owners. I fancied that we represented youth and youthful rebellion, which gave me at least, a distintinctly pleasant feeling. Of course, we would be looked at, askance, by the others, I told myself, age always feels mistrustful of youth; but now I'd found another; a horticultural sister-hood in the making, for support and mutual encouragement and easy-riding along the high-ways of Richmond Borough, Leisure Services. High Ho Silver and Away!

Chapter 7
A Hose Too Far

Proverb
*A man of words and not of deeds, is like a
garden full of weeds.*

At last my friend, fresh from camping in the Lake District
and during an interregnum before the Costwolds, took
pity on us both and bought a hose.

We gathered again on my living-room floor to put
together the nozzle parts which were bought separately. If
you're not familiar with these things, don't for one minute
imagine that using a hose is simply a case of Step One,
unroll-and-point-at grateful-plant. It took us a full twenty
minutes to work out how the various red, yellow and grey
bits of nozzle fitted together, even before we got anywhere
near the hose itself. It was worse than leggo and obviously
designed with the child in mind — unless you have been
raised on a diet of mega-drive computer games, don't even
think about it.

My friend shuffled off and I was left to launch the hose
on my own. I got up early one morning to "have a go". I
managed to find the hose, carefully hidden in the shelter
of scratchy brambles and with heaving and grunting, I
eventually managed to drag it out. It was tightly curled,
but still weighed a ton and looked as though, unfurled, it
would be very long, possibly even long enough to water
every other allotment in the place as well as our own.

I heaved it over to a rusty chair, sat down calmly and quietly and, while breathing deeply, tried to fit the nozzle. I was careful to take all these precautions for staying calm and in control because I am totally useless with anything requiring eye/hand coordination or of a faintly DIY nature. Painful and unpleasant experience has taught me, therefore, that I have to take these things slowly and never, never get upset, no matter what the provocation.

The moment, some half an hour later when, as if by magic, all the bits suddenly got bored with annoying me, and slotted into each other, was a profound one. I may have been hot and sweaty, but I had overcome.

I then made a truly fatal mistake and obviously celebrated too early, because no sooner had I then started to unwind the hose, when the entire length of it hurled itself into a complicated tangle and stayed there, unfriendly, uncooperative and sulking.

Hose is heavy. Meaning, that not only is it not light but it is not easy to manipulate. The amount of hose I was wrestling with, probably over three times what we actually needed, knitted itself up into a thrashing, heaving mass remarkably quickly and defied straightening. It mocked me. I was as incompetent to deal with its size and weight as those friendly Blue Peter presenters always look, when they are crazed enough to appear on live TV, with restless anacondas or baby elephants.

People came and went up and down the path where I fought this living thing alone; they shook their heads and smiled sympathetically, but there was nothing anyone could do to help — in the case of hose-pipe, many hands do not make light work.

I finally got the knots out and was left with just the kinks, so I decided to risk it and finally turned on the water. Nothing happened. This state of affairs continued until the exact moment when I raised the nozzle and gazed down it, to see if it was blocked. Then a fierce stream of suppressed water shot out and drenched my face, head and body within seconds. It was so cold I screamed, and I managed to drop the hose with the shock, whence it stayed to drench my legs and my shoes, until blinded by dripping water, I picked it up again and directed it, imprecisely, at some vegetables.

I could only be thankful that no one actually witnessed this part of the performance. I stood shuddering with shock and wet cold and went completely blank, or as blank as ceaseless and repetitive cursing will allow. Looking like a desperate candidate for the Wet T-Shirt competition and dreading that someone should see me, I dragged the hose down to the far end of the allotment until I'd dried off enough to appear in public again. Then, not to be completely outdone and for want of some more appropriate expression of my feelings, and of something better to do, I had a go at the hosing.

Despite feeling a complete idiot at having been reduced to an exhausted, wet clod by a garden implement, I found the actual business of hosing to be quite satisfying once I got going. I could see the earth turn from an unattractive greyish tinge to a rich, dark loam. The plants shook out their greenery and expanded in the drenching stream so as to catch even more of the water they had been wanting for so long. I walked among my beds, dispensing this largesse like a veggie god-mother granting wishes to veggie Cinderellas.

I called it a day when the hose got stuck round a screen of bean canes and threatened to bring the whole lot crashing down. Trying to wind the hose up again, proved to be just as bloody as the unwinding, so I finally resorted to kicking it into some sort of a bundle and dragging it behind the compost heaps. My friend was not going to be impressed with the state of her purchase.

Hosing threatened to be a perennial problem unless we/I could sort out how you made the thing behave.

Chapter 8
A Wet Wet Wet September

Proverb
A field requires three things; fair weather, sound seed, and a good husbandman.

After weeks of unprecedented and unBritish hot weather, the climate gods returned from their vacation and got down to some serious readjustment. It rained. On and on it went. One day it was all shorts and tank tops, the very next day I dug out my woolly bed socks, disgusting, paint and grease stained jogging pants and the final sartorial indignity, the great, shrunken once-cable-knit which had developed even more holes during the lay-off.

The partner absolutely hates that old sweater. For him, it symbolises everything mean, crooked and lazy about my nature. It also signifies a woman who has "stopped trying" — to please her man, him, that is.

I really can't see what his vendetta is all about. Why wear good clothes when you are just going to sit, alone, in front of a computer all day, enlivened by drinking coffee and evening trips to the lotty? The plants don't seem to care and as the weather, for two weeks, plunged itself into winter, offering grey skies, chill and drownpour — I dressed to save chillblains and overly frequent changes of clothes.

The ground became much, much easier though. Catching the occasional dry spell, I went at No 64 with a vigour which took me by surprise. It was so satisfying to feel the fork penetrate the surface of the ground, forcing downwards under my boot. Levering hard, backwards, to loosen choking grass and bind weed and heaving on the loaded fork to turn the heap and expose thick, heavy, black earth. My back ached and often my head swam, dizzy from all the effort I was willingly devoting to this labour.

Good, growing earth and worms were not all I exposed, of course. Earlier, dire warnings of endless blackberry roots came to pass. The roots were long, yellowish creatures often of a most astonishing length. My friend swears that one she finally tracked down to its lair, measured over two feet. I was not as rigorous as she in making sure that no vestige of the evil remained in the soil. Very often, I would abandon the effort to find the root of the root, as the wily things twisted and turned in the earth. After about a foot or so, if the enemy had not decently surrendered to my onslaught, I chopped it off with the spade, hoping that I had done enough damage to make it give up and stop growing. We'll have to wait and see if the strategy worked.

It really began to come home to me, also, just how big No.64 is. I dug and dug, making splendid progress. My friend did the same. Yet, coming up from the central path and looking up the whole length of the patch, our efforts were dwarfed by the still endless stretches of untamed wilderness.

True, I cannot ignore the fact that my friend's children made their contribution to the Clearance, by each digging a "wildlife pond". I almost missed them for the first two weeks of their existence. They were placed, side by side — not in the huge, naturally wildlife area which stretched over at least half of our patch — but in the flattened, ready-to-dig-and-hopefully-to-cultivate section, which had been burned off by Seamus. The kids were not fools.

The ponds are about a bucket size each in width and depth — one has dried up completely, despite the rain, the other sports a few bricks and a "bridge" plank. The wildlife will probably have to take turns in inhabiting the ponds, there's hardly room for more than one anorexic frog at a time. But, they are there and I believe my friend is proud of her kids' contribution.

We are generously bestowed with wildlife in our allotments. Being bounded by Richmond Park and Palewell Common and the well maintained spaces of the Bank of England Sport's Ground, no less, we get frequent visitors. There is a squirrel which bustles about in the tree at the bottom of No 64 and gives me a heart-attack every time (s)he makes a giant leap for rodent kind.

I'm usually bent double over another hoeing session, quiet and engrossed in the rapidly shading evening, consumed by the reflection that maybe just hoeing and leaving the weeds on the surface to rot down is essentially a lazy and fruitless task, as they just seem to grow back again, very quickly, and maybe I should be picking them all out by hand, like currants from a bun — and then, I'm shaken to the core as an almighty crash and racket to the rear, panics me into thinking, It's The Attacker! My blood pounds; I sweat and in those few seconds, I'm convinced that someone has burst through the fence, overcome by my female grace and beauty, and is going to get me — cable-knit and all. But, no, Squirrel has merely flexed its muscles and with small, perfectly formed polish, has taken off into the air or into the next tree or landed on the heap of rubbish shared by us and No 66.

My friend, however, can top my tales from Farthing Wood, because she has had the real pleasure of seeing a fox, basking in the sunshine, stretched out and at ease, on one of our sheets of net curtain which is meant to be protecting a mixed bed of rocket, spinach and endive.

The other wildlife not providing such warm pleasure is the "lads" from the school on the other side of the brook. Things have gone missing from the allotments round and about, not veggies but tools as substantial as wheel-barrows and my friend's very good wellies have disappeared among other items. My friend was really quite upset about the missing wellies. Not so much because of the things

44

themselves, smart though they had been, for wellies, but she felt that an element of confidence and trust had been broken. She felt that she would be looking at other allotmenters with the nagging suspicion that they might be the ones who had walked off with the boots. All their evident charm and friendliness would be forever tainted by her new doubt in them.

I must admit, I thought that taking her spanking wellies would have been a dumb move on the part of any of our lotty owners. They would be so easily recognisable that they could only have been worn in secret, or in the dark or given away for Christmas.

When, however, the lads began to Tarzan their way over the stream by slinging ropes across from "their" side to "ours", and swinging back and forth, with a lot less grace than the squirrel, the mystery was solved.

Research by concerned folk was judiciously conducted when the boys absented themselves — either because of the higher calls of learning or of supper — but their absence was vital, as nobody was keen to mess with these boys face to face, some of them looked well hard.

This research revealed that some of the missing items seemed to be on their side of the stream. It was further revealed that a raft had been built, ostensibly to navigate the brook and with this and repeated sessions of swinging across the water, it was obvious that wellies would be very handy.

My friend's faith in our allotment friends was thus happily restored.

The wellies could easily be sacrificed for that.

*

Proverb
*Patience is the knot which secures the seam of
victory.*

I had been seriously disappointed, yet again, this time by
the fact that none of the seeds I had planted had shown
any signs of life. Peas, kohlrabi, fennel all had failed to
germinate. I was crushed; a failure. I had been conscientious about following the instructions for each breed and
had gone to the extra trouble of net curtaining to ward off
flying attack; I had done my very best and that was not
good enough.

My friend was unconcerned at first, then rallied under
pressure, to share my set-back. She made enquiries on my
behalf and of our veg., while I moped and pretended to
ignore the problem. She enquired particularly of Valerie,
numero duo in the allotment hierarchy and officially
deputy to Eric, but really a supremo in her own right.

Valerie spends a goodly amount of time tending her
stretch, far more it seems than the 3.5 hours stipulated by
E.T.B. She is of medium height, grey hair sharply cut and
excellent figure — for a woman of her age (I unnecessarily
add, not knowing how old she is — she's probably younger
than me; her body certainly is.) I've seen this figure in
shorts and bikini top during the really, really hot weather
and pondered.

Her advice was that they should all have germinated by
now and that they didn't because of the extraordinarily
hot weather, despite all my attempts to keep the seeds
damp and that by now it was probably too late. All this,
meaning that my seeds had passed on, they were no more,
they had gone to seed heaven.

She also threw in, for good measure, the information
that all the tomatoes had probably split, again, because of
the dry weather, followed by quantities and quantities of
rain. Tomatoes go mad after such periods of prolonged
abstinence and greedily drink too much when the wonder-

46

ful wet arrives once more, and burst their very skins from over-indulgence. But, I suppose, like us, they would argue that they can't help themselves.

But then, a pleasant surprise grew from the ground, however. Under the wet onslaught of early September, the seeds shook themselves, returned from their out-of-body experience, reinhabited their husks and started to spring up green and healthy. Daily, under their net overcoats they grew bushy and confident, hustling to be thinned out, separated from each other and from the weeds which were challenging them for supremacy.

I was delighted, obviously, but I was surprised to find that none of the other allotments were showing young vegetable growth. I was puzzled that other people were duly turning their ground over and then leaving it — for the frost to do its work of breaking-down the clods and creating a useful tilth, or they planted a green manure to cover the area. No other allotment seemed to be keen to get in late peas, broad beans or my eagerly awaited fennel.

It was at a lunch party that I learned the truth.

Still struggling to maintain a semblance of social life, despite being reasonably newly poor and having two allotments to support, at social gatherings, I was beginning to notice that all people deemed it fit to talk to me about were the allotments. Questions on career progression and political affiliation were rarely addressed to me.

"Are you working at the moment?" asked Mark (nice guy, runs his own solicitor's firm with close friend and I was lunching with him, his sister, her new baby and its grandparents). "Yes, things aren't going too badly, all things considered," I hedged in reply.

That is such a difficult question to answer when you work for yourself; if the bailiffs aren't due round next week and you can pay half the bills on final demand, I judge things not to be going too badly.

"Is that work work or is that allotment work?" Mark spins back, in that semi-indulgent, semi-ironic tone I was becoming all too familiar with.

47

"Look I'm not Allotment Annie, you know," I countered sharply, "I do do other things than allotments. I do have a life."

Mark is too much of a gentleman to demand actual proof, but by then, I had set his Dad off anyway. Away we went on another allotment conversation. Not that he's got one, but he does grow his own veg. and lots of soft fruit so, as he said, it is an allotment in a sense.

According to him there is no real advantage in planting things to over-winter as they are hardly ready any earlier than if planted in the spring. The disadvantage is that they're subject to a rougher life what with the frosts and being the only foraging temptation around during the lean times of winter, for birds and mice. This is probably true, but being enthusiastic still, and hating the waste of all that unused growing space, my friend and I were happy to plant in the autumn even if we weren't very successful — we could always dig the growth back into the ground later, like a green manure.

*

What we were very busy with, at this time, was picking runner beans.

Chapter 9
More Runner Bean Soup, Anyone?

Proverb
Provision in season makes a rich house.

I know that it shouldn't have, but it did come as a shock when it happened. It shouldn't have, because surely that was the reason I took on first one, then two allotments in the first place? Yet, like most hobbies or pastimes, I happily invested time and effort (and money) in the allotments, for the sheer pleasure of it, never calculating the outcome, the "reward" for all the pains.

My extra-curricular activity was not glitzy or even trendy. I did not have to invest in an insurance policy to cover the risk to life and limb and there was no smart, expensive uniform to buy. Why bother? What was there to digging, weeding, hoeing *et al* that gripped and fired the imagination?

And then, the real prize in The Cultivation Game, revealed itself after the wet early September — and it came as a shock and a great delight.

We had veg.! Food grew. Real food, unpackaged, hand-picked, immediately present and there, in our ground, complete with roots and soil clinging to it. I was dizzy with how like the gardening programmes it all was. A townie by birth and upbringing, used to food in plastic — I was exhilarated by picking veg. The season of mists and mellow fruitfulness had come to life on our allotments.

We were frisky with the pleasure of it and convinced that we were stuffing ourselves with extra health and vitamins, with all the fresh, home grown produce we started to eat and getting brownie points from the respective partners who finally saw a real time pay-off.

The women, who, worryingly, had seemed to spend a lot less time around the family compound, catering to every need and whim, but getting up to who knows what among the vegetables, had come good at last. There was real, green food on the table, provided by the women; the men could get back to higher things.

Isn't extraordinary how the metaphors of tribal life hold good and strong in West London? Thank you David Attenborough.

*

Our courgette plants got a regular going over. I would pounce on an offering of a small, pencil-slim green finger of vegetable, with a huge yellow flower at its tip. Generally, I couldn't wait until it developed into a reasonable sized version, I would break it off and eat it there and then, endlessly engaging in the taste test. Was veg., straight from the ground sweeter, more tender than that killing time in shops? Usually, it was hard to tell with the courgettes; the timorous, little plants I had nurtured, had muscled out into four great, trailing monsters, sporting huge, prickly limbs and very little courgette, so few veg., in fact, that when I was lucky enough to spot one, it didn't seem worth while to save it for the table, much easier to eat it at once.

Our spinach was a pure joy. A lovely shade of pale green, perfectly formed spears of leaf with a taste quite unlike that of its tending-to-tough shop cousins. We even had a row of the trendy lettuce, rocket, that the magazines write about.

Until now, lettuce has meant nothing to me, other than as a green bulk-provider that you have with salad; tasteless and unremarkable, but there. Until rocket. A delicate plant, feathery with sculpted leaves and a tender white flower — until it hits your taste buds. Then, hot, peppery and more. A salad vegetable, needing nothing else to create smack-in-the-mouth pleasure.

I also went mad among the Swiss chard. Chopped down to within an inch of its life and stir-fried in olive oil with some random seasoning — I ate and ate and laughed at the days I used to hunt out an interesting green at the supermarket.

There were some fruits of our plot, and more particularly the fruits of Liam's earlier labour, that did not deliver quite so much elation value, however.

Liam had planted a whole bed of marrows. I managed to catch some of them, in their young, courgette phase, but delving about the thick growth, I would occasionally come across a dormant monster. These things seemed to lie low and silent, swelling beyond human or even vegetable proportions. I know that marrow is highly prized in some quarters, not only for its size and prize winning capability, but some people even like the taste.

In for a penny, in for a pound, and high on the success of other veg., I felt reckless and dared to have a go and cook and eat a marrow. Perhaps I was about to be surprised by joy.

The specimen lucky enough to be selected for this experiment was so heavy, I wheeled the bike around to transport it home. Its very weight was somehow uncompromising; I knew that it would brook no amateurs; that it would be completely unforgiving and that I would either get it exactly right and feast off marrow for a week, or the whole thing would be chucked in the bin — a tough, chewy, tasteless misfortune.

Faced with such a challenge, I decided that the partner was going to participate in the subjugation of this quite alien presence, which lay on the counter-top, yellow/green and taking up a lot of room.

He washed it down, carefully, and hacked out the measureless middle part, which was a mash of seeds and marrow mixed together, while I prepared the stuffing. We were not going to inject it with minced meat, so I boiled up pan loads of rice and mixed that in with onions, peppers, mushrooms, tomatoes, spinach and chard, all from the allotment bar the mushrooms.

Once prepared, we took it in turns to spoon this mixture into our hollowed out marrow. We had rests and cups of tea to alleviate this labour, as the whole exercise was stretching into the best part of a complete day. The partner then had the brain-wave of baking the whole lot over water, to create a steam, in the fragile hope that this would soften the outer skin.

He had not removed this item as part of the basic preparation. He had begun to do so, then got tired, when there was still about half a hectare of expanse to strip, so we had agreed to leave the skin on and eat the middle only, should the thing ever get cooked.

It did cook. It took a long time, but it did cook and we did eat it. Some of it. A giant, scooped out half of stuffed marrow, big enough (and tough enough) to navigate the Zambesi, palls after a while. The inside mixture was tasty, but we could have had that without the marrow.

The upshot was, that my friend and I took to giving marrows away to others whenever we came across them. Despite having to feed a family of four, my friend was of my persuasion regarding marrow — quite simply, why?

The outstanding crop of this period had to be the runner beans, though we were pleased with everything.

The beans, however, just did not stop coming up. Granted, we did have two sets of them. The biggest and most efficiently contstructed edifice being on No 70, where Liam had invested in a metal structure, over 7ft high on which he had grown extremely healthy and prolific beans for over 6 years. So much for the advantages of crop rotation, but more about that later.

On No 64, my friend had whipped up her own, less substantial cane arrangement to support "our" beans. For a while, we thought that neither set of beans was going to produce anything other than attractive red flowers. Either that or other people were helping themselves to Liam's beans behind our backs, as they were placed right next to the central pathway, conveniently acting as a screen to the rest of that plot, but very handy for straying fingers.

As for the lack of produce on No 64, they had been planted-up so late, that we really did not expect anything to happen anyway.

There had been a period of confusing interregnum after Liam first left for Sussex and before my friend and I could "officially" establish ourselves as being in possession of his plot. Liam's plot was highly desirable, well maintained and well planted and there was some muted feeling that perhaps some other, more deserving people could/should have taken occupancy. Whatever was around on that site, prior to our making it abundantly clear that we were now *in situ,* was probably considered free for all, including, so we thought, the beans.

We were very wrong. The beans started to crop on No 70 and once having got up a sufficient head of steam, beans seemed to sprout, long and fleshy, in clumps and in groups, in profligate abundance. We could not keep up with their productivity. Then, No 64 also made it to the starting line and we had beans in bagfuls.

I made a bean meal every day for about five days, then began to calm down, slowing my intake to three bean meals a week, leaving the surfeit to get forgotten in the back of the fridge. My friend went and filled her freezer with beans; took to leaving beans outside my front door, anonymously, and then started to way-lay other mothers on the school run, with "gifts" of bean bags.

I began to worry about waste and feel guilty about being sensitive that we always seemed to have so many more beans to deal with, no matter how many we ourselves ate or managed to palm off on others. I invented a bean soup,

53

that was not all that pleasant, but used up a lot of beans and felt better. The partner even had the nerve to complain, "not beans again!"

Chapter 10
The Finale of the Harvest Festival

Proverb
Zeal without knowledge is a runaway horse.

Towards the middle of October, our period of lavish abundance began to dwindle and dry up as if someone, somewhere, was turning off the supply tap. The plants were still in their beds in the ground looking generally healthy and leafy, but they were gradually withdrawing the favour of their wealth.

From experiencing an initial relief that the pressure of so much food to "deal with" was over, I soon began to miss our choice and variety.

It was true that the broccoli showed through at this time, but despite plants of a hugeness and size of leaf that of themselves, should have fed a village, the actual heads were meagre and sparse. Poor plant design I thought, most of the effort of growing the veg. was lost in extraneous green matter; it was like building a four storey house but having only the attic to live in.

I've since noticed that there are a number of vegetables that follow this pattern, mainly of the brassica family, things like brussels sprouts and cauliflowers and cabbages (in my plots, cabbage was one of the worst offenders in this brassica line). I had been somewhat unimpressed by the courgettes as well though, which, if we are being technical, fall into the category called cucurbits, after cucumbers.

Such plants must throw-back to their jungle ancestors, producing a flurry of great woody stems and huge tough leaves, fit for monkeys to dangle from and leaving almost no growth hormone left to spend on developing the heart of the matter, the bit we want to eat. Still, I continue to be encouraged if not amazed by any growth at all; if there is anything on a plant grown by me that I can actually eat as well, then that's just pure bonus.

I'm sorry to report that I was less than fair in the appropriation of what broccoli did grow. I took three small heads that I came across one day, during my hunt for something fresh, leaving nothing for my friend. And that proved to be it, the total harvest of broccoli which I'd nabbed — and my friend knew that I had.

This caused a small ripple in the fairly smooth pond of our communication. Generally, we had actually had no problem whatsoever in dividing the spoils. There had been plenty and each of us took what we wanted whenever we were down at the allotment. But, we were both partial to broccoli, rather especially as there was really only that and the chard and a bit of spinach left in our outdoor pantry. And I had whipped more than my fair share of this booty.

The situation over the broccoli had its good side, however, as it brought home to us that, for the next year, we would have to consult together over precisely what we would grow.

We would have to agree on how much of our available space we would devote to each kind of vegetable and, as importantly, how much we would spend on vegetable seeds and new fruit bushes. Once we got going, it didn't stop there. We fancied fig trees, apple trees, plums, not to mention exotica in the vegetable line that we thought we ought to try.

Our imaginations ran rampant over the seed catalogues, lingering over Chinese vegetables, artichokes and the like. We mentally had my friend's husband build fruit cages and numerous cold frames; we created wildlife, conservation areas and (proper size) ponds. We revelled in what we would do "next year" on our allotments.

We then took a reality check.

A lot of No 64 was still uncleared. I had been quite good at digging sessions, clearing the brambles and the elephant grasses, whilst my friend was heavily into the maintenance of No 70, weeding, digging up finished vegetables and planning — of this, more later.

More than half of No 64 remained, at best under carpet, at worst under varieties of man-sized weeds. My expectation was that I would continue to dig over the autumn and winter to provide growing space sufficient to transform our lavish blueprint into solid reality.

Life got in the way of this happy theory. I began to get busy at home-work. I foolishly started to try and relaunch my business around the end of September, which took up enormous amounts of time, energy and worry as well as that very scarce commodity — money.

I had begun to suffer the partner's slings and arrows. Not so much the abuse and accusations of not pulling my weight, but rather the huge self importance he was adopting as "provider". That really irritated me and spurned me on to get serious about earning a living.

This meant that I was home a lot, guarding the phone and not strolling down to the lotty to potter about with the best of the them. Time itself also conspired against me and my allotment work, by doing something with an hour during October, which meant that it was pitch dark by 4pm.

Now, I was reduced to week-end working and I seriously missed the opportunity for long, quiet evenings over my plants watching the day come to an end with the diminishing sounds of birds and tones of pink, dimming to darkness.

Evenings stretched out into the hibernation zone, nothing of nature to see from the windows except blackness and lines of car lights in traffic. For relief, there were other peoples' living rooms lit up like stage sets, if they forgot to draw their curtains; their lives acted out to my view, like soap operas without sound. Often and often I would turn on the TV, restless and with an enormous gaping evening to get through before bed time and the relief of day light once again.

Winter is not my best time.

My friend took to coming round for coffee. As I sat manning the telecommunications nerve centre for my business which I had established in the dining room, she would turn up with veggie offerings to cheer me up, coupled with regular up-dates on lotty news and views.

Of course her participation in what had been a joint venture rapidly outstripped my own. I found that she had literally discovered a new life in our allotments. I began to wonder what life had been like for her before we had Nos 64 and 70.

Her ideal day would consist of dropping her youngest off at school and making her way to the plots. Once there, she would try and spend until 3 pm, when she was forced to leave to pick the same youngest up from school.

Time disappeared for her on the allotments, interspersed with her sandwiches and coffee breaks. There is always something to do on an allotment, never mind two of them, but for her, the experience took on a far more meaningful significance than mere allotment management. She truly loved being on the allotment.

We talk about communing with nature, about being at one with something greater and more mysterious than ourselves and I think my friend found that to be true for her. Not in walking in some sunlit wood or contemplating a powerful ocean, but simply by pottering on the allotments.

She got so excited by her lotty love that she wanted to talk plants, soil construction, compost processing and plot management — a lot.

She read books on all the above, borrowed from the library and continually renewed. She listened to gardening programmes on the radio and watched TV on Friday nights when various channels compete for the attention of the week-end gardener. Her life was significantly changed by owning allotments, though gardening itself was not new to her as she had long had her own garden.

To be honest my own attraction was a pale, thin thing next to hers, in fact I was almost embarrassed, if not swamped by her zeal — how could I ever hope to keep up? I enjoyed our allotments as a part-time pastime. They were not the only subject on my mind and I was not always willing to spend Saturday at the allotment, when I could maybe go to the races instead.

I went through a period of guilt as I waited for the phone to ring in my nascent empire. I pictured her down on the plots, wrestling with turning and mixing the compost heaps with layers of manure, soil, kitchen waste and weeds and I wondered whether or not I should retire gracefully and leave her to it, communing with our slice of nature in her own way and free to do what and when she liked, without the bother of seeking my opinion and approval.

We eventually had to have a talk about the situation. Firstly, I discussed the position with Bernie, another all-dayer. Bernie had the same tendancy as my friend, wanting to spend all the hours of day-light tending her flowers, rather than her husband and her home. "He'll just have to get on with it," she insisted, cheerfully, "I love it here, I can't stand cleaning. I'd go mad if I stayed cooped up all day in the house."

I sympathised with her feelings. I felt that I was going slightly strange spending all the time alone at home, with the phone. Who said it was good to talk? Face to face maybe, but conversation, via the telephone, was no substitute for the sights, sounds and smells of Nos 64 and 70.

"Don't worry about it," advised Bernie, "she wouldn't spend so much time here if she didn't want to, she really loves it. I wouldn't feel guilty about it, if I were you."

Guilt being part of my religion, I was mollified but not convinced. I was glad, therefore, when my friend let me off the hook by, very delicately, referring to the pressure that I was under to make a go of my business and that she did not mind that I couldn't devote so much time to the allotments.

The trouble with allotmenting is that it is a social activity as well as just being a gardening one. Unlike gardening in your own patch of garden, which no doubt is delightful and chock full of contemplative enjoyment, half of the pleasure of owning an allotment is in meeting and chatting to the people you see regularly and you regularly see the same people.

The allotment brigade divides along lines of employment rather than age or sex. People with jobs (both sexes, not generally so young, nor so old) spend their evenings and week-ends catching up and "doing" their allotments, while retirees, married women and the army of the unemployed are free to wander our plots during the vast expanse of the day.

It is my contention, though by no means proven and will probably be hotly contested, that you can tell by the general state of order, neatness and productivity those plots owned by people who work for a living and have an allotment, from those who live to have an allotment.

*

As October saw an end to itself, the weather got colder and trips to the lotty became limited for everyone else as well as me, my friend called a meeting to discuss crop rotation and to decide on which method of the same we would adopt for the future husbandry of our future veg.

Chapter 11
November and December

Proverb
*Those who aim at the moon may hit the top of
a tree; those who aim at the top of a tree are
unlikely to get off the ground.*

We duly met one Sunday afternoon at my friend's house
when her family were off doing other things.

It was particularly wet and cold this day, though parts
of November had been a delight with bright, bright blue
skies and a clear cold which clears the lungs rather than
congests it with colds and flu.

I wandered in expecting some cosy veg. chat, nothing too
stretching and more social than serious.

Did I happen to mention that another of my friend's
qualities is that she is an ace at Maths? She sees numeri-
cal relationships where others merely see a few squiggles
on a page. Unbeknownst to me, my friend had been doing
some planning work around our allotments. The answer to
my earlier musing as to what she found to do when the
weather was so inclement that there was no digging/weed-
ing work to be done, was that, not to be separated from her
plots, she drew them.

Not for her, however, a fine sketch in charcoal maybe or
an accomplished gouache reproduction (she'd leave that to
our artist friend Jane for the summer). No, my friend had
been down to Nos 64 and 70 complete with graph paper,

industrial tape measure and pencil. The result was a fairly close plan of each of our plots, in metres and centimetres what's more (which I still cannot get to grips with). These plans showed where various veg. lay, the width and length of plots and paths and, for No 64, where the major obstacles were, like the ash and elderflowers.

I was stunned and impressed. I was also slightly wondering why she had gone to all this trouble. I am of the *laissez-faire* school of life and gardening. I do not seek to create things to do for myself, when there seems to be so much around to do anyway.

My friend, however, filled me in.

We were both continually irritated when we tried to manoeuvre ourselves around No 70 because though, as I have said, it is really well laid out in permanent beds, with wooden borders, Liam obviously wanted to eke as much growing space out of the plot as he could, when under his management, because the paths were squeezed to an absolute minimum.

Often as we gingerly put one foot in front of the other down one of his paths, anxious to avoid stepping on the bed itself for fear of disturbing the structure of the soil, a sin which Liam had preached hotly against, I, particularly, would just topple over, unable to keep by balance. My size 8 boots would entangle themselves and I would end up landing on anything from veg., and canes to mud and manure. My infrequent trips to the lotty during these months, usually resulted in me having to come home and throw absolutely everything I had on into the wash, followed by myself into the bath.

My friend and I had talked about changing the bed layout to accommodate bigger paths, which, according to her, we could plant with grass sods (obtainable from skips) and keep tidy by mowing. As for No 64 it did need serious planning attention because it was too *al fresco* for serious cultivation. Still half uncleared, ponds *et al* and an eclectic assemblage of veg. which we had thrown in before the last season ended, it was ripe for redevelopment.

So, she had got right down to it, put it on paper and with the clear knowledge of each plot's overall length and width, which we had never had before, we got down to redesigning it.

I was some help during this process. It was me who suggested we start from the river end on No 70, as the raspberry bushes there were well past their sell-by date and needed to be dug up. I felt the same about the rhubarb which came next, and as following that plot, there were two empty sections, which had recently been home to potatoes, we had more free space to start redesigning.

I agreed to dig up both raspberries and rhubarb, but leave the more accurate activity of measuring and marking the new plot areas to my friend.

We then got down to the nitty gritty ie deciding which crop rotation scheme to follow.

I know about crop rotation like I know about quantum physics, that is, it's there, it has being, it exists in a universe parallel to, but not intimate, with my own. Well, of course, my friend was on far more familiar terms with the entire subject.

The general idea is to keep closely related vegetables together in veggie ghettos, moving them, *en masse* to a different patch of ground each year, so that they don't get back to where they started from for three or four years. No settling down, getting the feel of the place and establishing roots, for vegetable life. No, because these very roots are likely to develop diseases in the soil and horrible-sounding pests like eelworm, if left over too many years. The soil, itself, needs to be given a break from repeatedly growing one sort of crop, which drains it of one set of nutrients and can leave it exhausted.

Doesn't this remind you of certain members of your family? The brother who never has any money and is always draining you of spare cash. The sister who exhausts you with endless conversations about the boyfriend.

It continues to surprise me how anthropomorphic the growing life can be. Particularly when we began to discuss cycles, not of the moon, which I now expected, but what we dubbed the, normal cycle and the "alternative" cycle of crop rotation.

Vegetables are generally grouped according to whether they are brassicas, potatoes, peas and beans or onions. What veg. meet in which group is determined by what kind of dining experience they enjoy, or to put it more technically, what soil and nutrients they require. I was not, for example, expecting to find that leafy broccoli could be grouped with the more solid kohlrabi in the brassica family, just because they both like the nitrogen left by legumes. Potatoes, courgettes and sweetcorn, three very varied things to eat, can settle together because they, too, like the same conditions ie heavy feeding. (Images of hefty lorry drivers and hairy road diggers eating large fry-ups in a road-side cafeteria spring to mind?)

My friend said that we must decide which scheme we would follow because it would obviously affect our management routines for at least four years to come. We could go "normal" or "alternative", according to her reading.

Something inside me screamed for anything normal, if only in the gardening line, so fractured did living strike me then, but I resolved to put emotions aside and carefully examine the pros and cons of each method.

"Normal", the term which we gave the crop rotation scheme which most of our books described, means that, firstly, you divide your available space into four, equal areas. You then usually then further subdivide these areas into beds.

In each of the four equal areas, or plots, vegetables would be grown, in rotation in something like the following manner: in Year 1, plot 1 would be devoted to peas and beans, plot 2 would have brassicas, plot 3 potatoes and tomatoes and plot 4 would have root vegetables. In the following years, the vegetables in each plot would be rotated.

The other cycle, however, would have brassicas in plot 1

64

in Year 1, potatoes in plot 2, peas and beans in plot 3 and
only get back to "normal" in plot 4, which would also be
devoted to roots and onions.

My analytical friend, who had all of this information off
pat in her head, thankfully got as tied up as I was by now
feeling, trying to explain these systems to me. Basically,
the schemes come down to this:-

"Normal" Cycle

Yr	Plot 1	Plot 2	Plot 3	Plot 4
1	Peas/beans	Brassicas	Potatoes	Roots/onions
2	Brassicas	Potatoes	Roots/onions	Peas/beans
3	Potatoes	Roots/onions	Peas/beans	Brassicas
4	Roots/onions	Peas/beans	Brassicas	Potatoes

"Alternative" Cycle

Yr	Plot 1	Plot 2	Plot 3	Plot 4
1	Brassicas	Potatoes	Peas/beans	Roots/onions
2	Potatoes	Peas/beans	Roots/onions	Brassicas
3	Peas/beans	Roots/onions	Brassicas	Potatoes
4	Roots/onions	Brassicas	Potatoes	Peas/beans

Let me say now that I never did grasp why there is a difference in the two systems. I believe that on some occasion
during that long, long winter afternoon, my friend must
have hauled out at least five books, and tried to scramble
through the fog in my brain. She did surely try to get me
to appreciate the fine distinction between these cycles and
why one or other of them should be preferred for one or
other of our plots.

What happened during that afternoon, apart from my losing the will to live, was that we may or may not have made a decision about crop rotation but time alone will tell, because I don't know. Pyschoanalysts would probably say that I am in denial over the issue. So be it.

I like gardening, but I deeply appreciate why, superficially, it may appear dull to others. Gardening is a sport which, I think, can only really be appreciated in the doing. Reading about the technical aspects of gardening, if you've never had the real pleasure of growing flowers or vegetables or anything else, must be as animating as a careful description of tiddlywinks.

I look forward to having the benefits of careful crop rotation revealed to me as I practise it; right now, I take it on faith that it will make a big difference. Certainly it's going to make identification all the easier during the growing stages of our putative veg. Come June, I can hear myself saying to my friend, as we peer at something, "If this is Year 1, bed 2 then these must be broccoli."

*

These winter months demonstrated that over-wintering vegetables did not give such a head-start in production. The peas I'd planted late, all expired and we didn't have much better success with the mooli. On the plus side, our kohlrabi, once thinned looked like it would survive these really cold winter months and the great surprise was that even the fennel, which I had transplanted into individual pots and put into an improvised cold frame, seemed to be hanging in there.

In general, we think that we would have been better advised to sow more green manures, like most of our fellow allotmenters, but earlier than we did. Not until the beginning of November did we get round to sowing winter tares and a winter field beans on the beds which had previously held potatoes on No 70. The ground here is really heavy and only gets the sun in the second half of the day.

My strongest motivation for sowing these potential manures was, yet again, to avoid hard work, later on. I hoped that they would provide good weed cover over the winter and that they would refine some of the really heavy lumps of clay which made up these beds, thus making preparation of the ground, next spring, a light, enjoyable task rather than a back-breaking one.

There were no signs of growth of our green manures for ages after planting and that which finally showed through was a bit sparse and not the bushy, vigorous green cover that we had been hoping for. Still, every little helps.

On the odd days that the weather did allow, my friend got down to double digging the patch of No 64 which I had largely single dug in the autumn. Apparently this was not an easy task for her, as she quickly discovered that, as I had dug, I had not cleared the ground of blackberry roots, that I had done something of a cosmetic job and left whole feet of root lurking in the ground. "It's no good leaving them there," she said as to nobody in particular, while I went slightly pink and tried to look nonchalant, "because we don't want new, blackberry bushes springing up all over the place and in between our potatoes, do we?"

Of course we didn't.

Chapter 12
The New Year.

Proverb

Yule is come and Yule is gone, and we have feasted well; so Jack must to his flail again, and Jenny to her wheel.

"The short days of winter are perceptibly lengthening, and birds are already pairing up in preparation for nesting: magpies are inspecting last year's nests, and the sound of the industrious wren wakes me long before dawn as she searches for spiders in my own back garden. Although it seems ages until spring activity quickens, if you wish to put up a bird box don't delay, for as in our housing market desirable properties are much sought after."

The Allotment Naturalist. Barnes Horticultural & Allotments Society Newsletter — January.

The days were perceptibly lengthening, as our own Naturalist reported. The gloomy grey of evening lengthened its tail gradually from 4 to 4:30 and then 5pm before finally reaching the fullness of its winter pitch, giving a whole extra hour of "living" time.

For those intrepid enough to venture down to the allotments and brave the bitter wind, which bore down directly on East Sheen from Siberia (literally), there was important, even feverish, activity.

For the month of January only, there was that small window of opportunity for members of the B.H.A.A.S. to decide which seeds to order from the shed in order to qualify for the highly advantageous discount available through bulk-purchase. Then there were the onion and shallots to buy (two varieties of each) that were in and would "go" quicker than the first day of the Harrods' sale and, finally, there were potatoes to order — again, all at a good discount.

People were also lavishly buying and spreading large amounts of mushroom compost to feed their beds, which we didn't do because we were still uneasy about the infamous crop rotation scheme. We wanted to buy this compost, because everyone else was buying so much of it that it was obviously a key factor in vegetable success. But, we felt that if we made a move in the direction of composting any bed, then, sods law dictated, that that would end up being the very bed which should not have received any compost this year because it was due for carrots.

Growing a good carrot is the bane of any novice gardener's life and so, quixotically, her one true goal. So much can blight the development of your simple carrot, I am now in awe of the fact that there are lots of them around and that they are viewed as ordinary to the point of being commonplace.

Ignoring the villanous, root-ruining carrot fly which like any proficient intercontinental ballistic missile, flies around until it hones in on the scent of growing carrot and gorges itself to the immature carrot's destruction. The carrot doesn't do much to help itself either.

My caring, nurturing tendancies, learned in the North and resulting in a fat childhood, dictate that I lavishly feed anything which I want to thrive and develop, including, therefore, my veg. But carrots, like teenage girls, have their own agenda and according to their faddy eating habits, fork and skew into mocking, deformed parodies of the traditional wedgy pencil shape, if provided with tasty, nutritious, scrummy, fresh compost or manure.

The vexed question of the crop rotation scheme was proving to be something of a sword of Damocles hovering like a personal rain cloud, over my head. Lost in ignorance and secretly impatient of the whole thing, (I find one does tend to scorn what one doesn't really understand) on my odd visits to the lotty, to dig up the rotting remains of the Swiss chard and finally clear the old rhubarb bed, I walked around a bit lost. I didn't know what to do, or what I could do which wouldn't be in conflict with the cursed eventual rotation scheme.

*

Out of spite, when there was so much digging still to be done, the weather turned nasty bringing severe frosts, snows, trouble-at-mill and ground too hard to work.

Concern about the state of the weather had become an even greater addiction during my short period of allotment ownership, from the preoccupation normal for your average Briton. Being cold or wet or too hot had consequences beyond the impact on my personal fashion statement and the daily, "Shall I take an umbrella today or not?" which was the invariable last shot from the partner as he left for work.

Reports on the radio, on the TV and in the papers fed the need-to-know almost hourly. Despite this barrage of weather information, which, during these months, almost without fail translated, in gardening terms, into "if you go down to the allotment today, you'll freeze every moving part in your body", it retained its fascination and I became a weather junky.

During a particularly severe patch in our worst winter for football since 1963, a useful meteorlogical statistic provided by Radio Four, one of my weather favourites, my friend and I got together to decide how to spend money legitimately. What were we going to grow in our first year of complete allotmenting?

What seeds were we going to buy?

Assembling at my commercial H.Q., it took two meetings to sort this one out.

We wanted everything and we wanted it now.

Which included a lot of potato-space for my friend. Eating a lot of potatoes and spending a lot of money on them, she thought it sensible to grow them.

I was not in the same place.

I had weaned the partner, gradually, from the inordinate love of potatoes which was bred into him with mother's Irish milk. Thickening waist lines and heavy hams decreed, according to me, that we go easy on the carbohydrate fest and eat more "green" veg. instead.

The problem was that we only had about 20-21 beds in total, 13 on No 70 and about 8 on No 64 which we would actually clear this year. I felt that devoting 3 whole beds soley to my friend's potato needs, with me wanting about 1 potato bed, meant that rather a lot of space was used up. What about all the other "interesting" veg? Would we have room for my varied selection of Chinese vegetables for example?

My friend appreciated my feelings and so in the spirit of compromise, we took to bargaining over space allocation, using beds like chips in a poker game. I would trade her 3 beds against an extra bed over which I would have jurisdiction and if there were any vacant space after the main allocation, I would decide how we used it.

We came away flushed and satisfied after our gritty negotiation.

What we decided to grow, the varieties of each and how much space we eventually allotted, is shown below. As you can see, we managed to accommodate all our veggie needs and wants — on paper anyway.

Vegetable	No. Beds	Variety
Potatoes	4	1st early — Pentland Javelin
		2nd early — Wilja
		Maincrop — Desiree
Onions	1	Shenshyu
		Stuttgarter
		Red Braums
Shallots		Golden Gourmet
Garlic	*To be*	*"fitted in"*
Carrots	1	Amsterdam Forcing (round/early)
		Autumn King 2
Beans Runner	1/2	Enorma
French	1/2	Blue Lake (Climbing/haricot)
		Royalty (Dwarf/purple)
Broad	1/2	Aquadulce (planted '95)
Peas	1	Kelvedon Wonder (Early/Main Crop)
		Sugar Dwarf Sweet Gem (Mangetout)
Turnip	1/2	Golden Ball (Maincrop)
Swede	1/2	Ruby
Spinach	2/3	Sigma Leaf (Summer)
		Perpetual Spinach (Hardy)
Chard	1/3	Silver
Kale	1/3	Thousand Headed (Plain leaf)
Courgettes	2/3	Burpee Golden Zucchini
Celery	1/3	Tall Utah 5270 Triumph (Self blnch)
Leeks	11/2	Autumn Giant 3 — Rami
Brussel Sprouts	1/3	Bedford Winter Harvest
Broccoli	1	Nine Star Perennial (Spring)
		Autumn Spear (Autumn)
Cabbage	1	Durham Early (Spring)
		Red Durham (Red variety)
		January King 3 (Winter maturing)
Cauliflower	1/2	Walcheren Winter 3
Parsnips	1/3	The Student
Celeriac	1/3	Balder

Salad Crops

Vegetable	No. Beds	Variety
Tomatoes	11/2	Sungold (Cherry variety)
		Marmande (Beef variety)
		Tigerella (Stripped variety)
		F1 Incas (Plum type)
Capiscum	1/3	World beater
Fennel	1/2	Planted in '95
Lettuce	1	Rocket
		Endive
		Mixed Lettuce
		Windermere (Iceberg variety)
Radishes	1/3	French Breakfast 3
Beetroot	1/3	F1 Pablo
Cucumber	1/3	Bush Champion
Parsley	1/2	Favorit
Basil	1/4	Bush Basil
Coriander	1/4	Coriander
Oregano	1/4	Oregano

We plundered the seed catalogues to produce this list, on the way, drinking in the names by which vegetables are christened. Mellifluous as Yeats' verse, these names grace the vegetable they identify, because gardeners have souls steeped in the romantic — a fact challenged by the common view of gardeners, which sees us as being all dirt and earth worms. But these sceptics should consider the seed catalogues, the literary canon of the gardening fraternity to discover therein the true world of imagination and description.

In our growing future, we would be munching not a lowly runner bean, but a "Royalty" or a "Blue Lake". Our kale would be "Thousand Headed" and our carrots,

"Autumn King". It turned out that our celery would likely be "Tall Utah 5270 Triumph", which rather broke the spell, but there is also a lot of poetry which is, frankly, incomprehensible.

Just as frustration with crop rotation was about to become total, my friend sorted it all out for us. Apparently she took to solving the problem instead of devouring detective novels, her former nightly bed-time reading.

I think it requires the same mind-set, so that if you are good at cross-word puzzles and always spot the perpetrator before Inspector Morse (a firm favourite), you've got a fair chance of being comfortable with CR. (Yes, there is another word which begins with these two letters and I used it mostly to describe the other two.)

Rather than spend more time boring you with it, what you can see below is how the vegetables we had decided to grow for in our new year, separated into the four families.

VEGETABLE FAMILIES

Peas/Beans	Brassicas	Roots/Onions Potatoes/Tomatoes

Beans

Broad	Brussels	Beetroot — Capsicum
Dwarf	Broccoli	Early Carrots
		Jerusalem Artichokes
French	Cauliflower	1st Early Potatoes
Runner	Cabbage	Parsnips

Peas

Early	Kale	Salsify
Main	kohlrabi	Scorconera
Mangetout	Mooli	Chives
	Radish	Garlic
	Spring Greens	Leeks
	Swede	Japanese Onions
	Turnip	Maincrop Onions
		Spring Onions

Other Main Crops

Spinach		Celery Courgettes
Spinach Beet		Celeriac Cucumber
Swiss Chard		Marrow
		Pumpkins
		Sweetcorn

Catch Crops

Chicory, Endive, Lettuce, Rocket

The "catch crops" are those which we would "fit in" around growing our other vegetables.

The next job was to sort our bed system into those which would be devoted to each family and we decided to do this on an ABCD rotation. This meant that we would have a complete rotation every four rows of beds, thus, bed A would be roots and onions for example, bed B would be brassicas, bed C peas and beans and bed D potatoes.

We decided to split our rotation in this way, in order to minimise the risk of four, entire beds developing one pest, which would be more likely to happen if we grew roots and onions in one set of four beds, potatoes in another clutch of four etc. etc.

Well, now that that was out of the way, we both felt a lot happier and more confident, as though we had just discovered the real meaning of life and we still had time to enjoy it before the sky caved in.

My friend then raced away and produced more plans, this time relating the beds in No 64 and Liam's plots to our new, planned system. If the agricultural commisariat of the former communist block had had my friend's help, *perestroika* would probably never even have got a look in.

No 64

Rotation Plan For New Year

Bed	What grown before	Peas/beans	Brass-icas	Roots	Pot-atoes
	PATH				
1	Herbs/weeds	+			
2	Weeds		+		
3/4	Weeds/rhubarb				+
5	Brambles/elderfl/weeds		FRUIT		
6	Weeds/brambles/nettles				+
7	Weeds	+			
8	Burnt area/weeds		+		
9	Weeds			+	
10	Weeds				+
11	Spinach/beans	+			
12	Toms/courge/beans		+		
13	Capsicum/toms/kale			+	

Liam's

	PATH				
1	Spr.cabb/beans/onions				+
2	Fennel/peas/beans	+			
3	Kohlrabi/peas/leeks		+		
4	Strawbs/chard		STRAWBERRIES		
5	Chard/cabb/onions/leeks			+	
6	Toms/leeks/beet/chard				+
7	Marrows	+			
8	Peas/potatoes/toms		+		
9	Potatoes/toms			+	
10	Potatoes/rhubarb				+
11	Leeks/kale/spinach	+			
12	Rasps/leeks/kale/spin.		+		

You may have spotted as you glanced, with a profound yawn, at the above, that what we had been able to grow on No 64 so far, largely consisted of weeds. This crop we were good at. We had also acquired an A Level in brambles. But, we were not even close to a certificate on most of the produce that seemed to litter the plots of almost all our allotment neighbours.

During these winter months, I gazed, salivating, at the fine, fat leeks that almost everybody else had in abundance on their sites. Our leeks, of which we had quite a few dotted over both plots, were skinny, wimpish things which refused to grow fat and prosper. They looked sick and resentful, blown about by the winds and covered by the snows. I rather wished that they'd do us a favour and just die off, so that we could get on with the job of changing the bed sizes at Liam's, but they hung on to life, out of spite, of no good to me or any of the foraging wildlife which must have been short of a good meal during the dreadful weather. Even desperation, though, couldn't make them to eat our leeks.

This was the lean season.

The local supermarkets had picked up my trade in vegetables again because we had so little to eat of our own. But this year, we vowed things would be different. We swore that we would be eating home grown all year round and that we would be so rich in yield that we would sell the excess to friends to pay for the following year's seeds and compost.

Proverb
Experience keeps a dear school, but fools
learn in no other.

Chapter 13
February

Chinese Proverb
You cannot prevent the birds of sadness from flying over your head, but you can prevent them from nesting in your hair.

The TV gardening programmes recovered from a dependency on films of gardens shot in the heat of summer or tours through tropical gardens in lush foreign regions. They had been intent on feeding us sufferers of digging-deprivation with memories of how it was or how it could be again, while we endured the interminable winter.

Half way through February, tele-gardeners were propelled back to real-time with a bump and were treated to shots of snow-covered areas and barren plots, just like their own at home.

The presenters didn't stay outdoors for long, however. Apart from a brief introduction and attractive camera work of frozen wastes, the paid experts ushered themselves rapidly indoors to conduct the real business in what looked like palatial green-houses.

These temples-to-growth came complete with equipment to rival NASA, but what particularly caught my attention were the heat pads on which you place young seedlings. Along with automatic temperature and humidity control, watering systems and sterilised containers, the natty electric under-blankets encourage the seedlings to get veg. off to a strong and early start.

And so I should jolly well think. Any living thing which had that much time and money spent on it should be developing beyond the evolutionary limits set out by Darwin or be giving darn good reasons why they'd fallen short of the mark.

My seeds were still firmly in their packets awaiting the spontaneous work of nature to prepare ground warm enough to bed them out in. Any plant pots I owned counted themselves lucky if they saw hot soapy water between plantings, never mind sterilising equipment and as for watering, we had made a giant leap into the 19th century by buying the hose-pipe.

Not to be off-put and keen to be doing, we began to organise the bed sizes on No 64 and to reorganise the bed sizes on Liam's.

This was fun and felt like mature, adult work complete with yellow marker string and tape-measure. Very rapidly, both plots were decked-out with odd pieces of wood, twig or rusty pipe holding lines of yellow string about 3" above the earth, so much so that Liam's plot took on the nature of a giant-child's game of cat's cradle. The overall effect could be a bit confusing, so I had to concentrate hard sometimes to work out what was marked-out as bed and what as path.

Next, we decided to have a good look at the compost.

We had been assiduous in our attempts at developing a good, organic compost. All the books vaunted the benefits to be derived from making one's own which would help to provide us with healthy, fertile soil as well as an outlet for all the green, veggie rubbish invariably left from weeding or digging over a bed.

On Liam's plot, the great man had left us with two, big wooden slatted structures which we began to fill with weeds and vegetable refuse just as the books said and they looked very much the business.

On No 64, things were a little more *a la rusticana*. We began to leave our offerings more or less on the same spot, more or less covered by a few sheets of plastic. Obviously this quickly began to look like a dumping ground rather than the tribute to organic gardening that it was intended to be. Bits of orange peel, potato peelings and, the almost inevitable, grape-fruit halves would break free of confinement and be seen rolling around the path and littering the weeds or the plastic would be blown off the top of the pile in the wind and the entire heap would disengage itself and sink and sag and look miserable.

I am proud to say, that I took this matter in hand and constructed a corral out of pieces of abandoned cupboard door which we had pressed into service to see off some of the weeds on No 64. With even this attempt at a boundary, the compost heap took on a new lease of life and began to decompose a little bit as if to show willing. Overlaid with a touch of guinea-pig bedding-cum-droppings from my friend's pets and we soon had a genuine heap of something quite like.

I had a system worked out for collecting vegetable matter from home to aid our compost expansion. I placed a plastic bucket on full view in the kitchen, lined with a plastic carrier bag into which I chucked tea leaves (used), coffee grinds and vegetable peelings.

I left it in full view of all comers to the kitchen, not by way of *avant garde* sculpture, but to remind me and the partner to put organic left-overs in it and not in the main bin. He never somehow got the hang of this simple requirement and I was ever elbow deep in Marigold gloves in the bin, fishing out wet tea-leaves and old carrot peelings, anxious not to loose a drop of valuable potential goodness.

The main reason this kitchen compost bin was left out though, was to remind me to take it down to the allotments — regularly — because all that precious organic matter left around in a warmish kitchen soon developed a smell to rival a horse's backside after feeding-time.

The other main constituent of our compost heap was horse manure.

The riding stable nearest me and our plots sells horse manure at 50p for a big, bin bag size, as long as you collect it yourself. One day during the summer, my friend and I collected six bags of the stuff. These felt like a prized possession. We left them at Liam's to rot down a bit so that we could add the manure to the compost. Unless horse manure is left to "mature" it is such a powerful material that it can scorch the plants you want it to feed and cherish, so it has to be handled with respect. Unlike my friend, I was not tempted to handle it at all and conducted the entire procedure with my trusty, industrial-strength, rubber gloves on.

I did make the mistake of collecting the manure wearing only trainers though and for months afterwards, horse by-product was stuck fast in those complicated groove-patterns that decorate the soles of even the cheapest trainers and I tracked a faint but definite smell of horse around for some time.

We eventually got round to creating a proper heap by turning out all the material we had gathered and then putting it all back again, but this time in layers. A layer of grass cuttings, followed by a layer of vegetable cuttings, followed by a layer of manure and then soil and then so on again. Hefty work, which eventually produced a terrine-like effect of different coloured and textured layers. This was then topped with old newspapers and carpet, to create warmth and to generate heat which turns all the various components into common, black, friable compost. The entire creation was then topped off with plastic to keep out the wet.

All this had been three or four months ago and as we were debating whether or not to invest in mushroom compost, I suggested we have a decko at the stuff we had made earlier, to see if it was ready and would do instead.

Armed, once again, with the mega-gloves without which I did nothing on the allotment, we carefully peeled back the layers of padding. Once we'd pulled off the plastic and carpet we found that the newspaper had got suitably damp, soggy and in a state compatible with the creation of *papier-mâché* models. This gave us much encouragement. What might not have happened to the real compost if the crisp, bright newsprint had undergone such a transformation?

Well, almost.

The mixture underneath was semi-cooked. It still had large pieces of identifiable plant in it; it had developed worms which came as a shock to me, but were exactly along the desired lines and most of the different ingredients had more or less broken down to become compost. It didn't look enough like the stuff you buy in garden centres to really convince me that it was true compost. And it obviously didn't convince my friend either, because, she soon persuaded me that we should buy some sterilised mushroom compost — anyway.

We bought four bags that day, encouraged, as I said, because everybody else was keenly purchasing it and squirrelling it away on their plots.

But very soon after, we were talking about buying another 16 bags.

I'm not sure what we will do with our own version now. Have we reached compost-overload? Have we made our own compost redundant? Does compost keep? Does it matter?

*

On a day, towards the end of the month, I just couldn't take it any more. I abandoned my phone-watch and hordes of clamouring clients; packed a picnic lunch of two, cold, old croissants and the left-overs of a turnip and brown rice feast which had been doubtful when first produced, but now, several days older had even to less to recommend it, filled the flask with tea and went down to the allotment.

It was a Wednesday. Always a day set apart from the

general trend of week days, as though the headlong rush of the week has temporarily put the brakes on around its middle period, collecting enough breath to continue the charge through to the island of the week-end. This change around Wednesday, is probably most noticeable in the suburbs rather than in the intensely commercial city centres, because many local shops still choose to have a half day closing and educational establishments, both junior and senior seats of learning, go play games in fields.

The 'burbs take a bit of a breather.

My decision to let all go hang, had been prompted by a sudden burst of warmth which had sprung out from behind steel grey skies and a bitter wind around 12:15pm. *Carpe diem.*

I made myself comfortable on one of the red, plastic chairs which were looking even shabbier and rustier than ever, thank heavens — safe from rip-off.

I got out my lunch and sat and ate and enjoyed. It was quiet. There was no one else in view. Even the planes on the relentless path to Heathrow seemed more muted during this period. A bird came out and sang for me above the general chatter of its friends and I surveyed my domain.

Things were looking bleaker at No 64. So much had been cut back, so much carpet had been laid that there was now hardly any of the lush, wanton rampant growth of six months earlier.

My friend's husband had given the shed a new, green felt roof and fixed its door. The intrusive vine had been stripped away from the shed's interior and all the shelves were neatly ranged to accommodate hoardings of newspaper, plastic bottles, plastic bags, bits of wood and the other paraphernalia of "The Borrowers" school of gardening, apart, that is, from actual tools. These were well hidden in case of vandals.

More than half of No 64 was now dug over. The yellow lines of string, marking putative bed from path, lent an air of serious intent to this section. Beyond this area, carpet took over in its role of weed suppressant and I spotted the addition of an old door and some extra cupboard parts newly arrived off some skip or other since my last visit.

I missed the old No 64. I had liked its abundance and the sense of privacy all that renegade green had lent to the plot. Obviously things were much more utilitarian and ready for gardening action now, but the scene had lost a lot of its magic for me and No 64 had become much like many other allotment sites seen from the window of a passing train.

My musings with nature were interrupted as normal weather was resumed, grey clouds began to form and the odd spot of rain bit me on the cheek.

With a great sigh, I packed away my lunch, dished the dregs of tea and went to exhume the fork from its hiding place. There was still work to be done after all and I was hoping to finish clearing and double-digging a bed before the weather got its grip on the day and put paid to any attempt at allotment work on my part.

I wasn't yet ready to go back to the telephone.

Chapter 14
March

Proverb

When Easter Day lies in our Lady's lap, then,
O England, beware of a clap.

The seed potatoes we had ordered were late in coming through but we would still have to leave them to sprout before attempting to plant them out whenever they finally made it.

This was going to be an interesting exercise because we had ordered 12 pounds of seed potatoes in total and the rules say that they should be laid out in something like egg-boxes, sprouting side uppermost — until sprouted or chitted, as we experienced gardeners like to say.

I live, quite comfortably, in a two-bedroomed flat and my friend has her house cosily filled with a husband, two children and two guinea-pigs. We were going to find it logistically stretching to make room for potato sprouting as well, even if we crammed them onto every available surface, including bath and beds. It would probably be easier to turn the living-room into a battery farm and "chit" chickens.

People on the allotments were getting excited about the approach of spring. Not that the weather was providing much of a clue, but the days continued to lengthen, the seeds arrived at the allotment trading shed and people, not seen for weeks, began to appear on their plots, digging furiously in a last minute rush to get their beds ready for planting.

One grey, late afternoon early in the month, I was working up a lather grubbing out yet more bramble roots on No 64, when George came up and introduced himself. I was delighted to stop for a chat.

"You're the friend aren't you?" he asked. He lit what looked like a roll-up, but probably wasn't. He was probably smoking ordinary cigarettes, but I felt he suited the image of a roll-up man more. He wore an interesting blue, woolly hat perched on the top half of his head and I noticed that he had serious gardener's hands.

I had seen George around quite a bit. He and his wife, Betty, were allotment regulars, who were victims of the expansion of the local school play-ground which was taking a slice of the top section of the allotment site. Those people unlucky enough to have their allotments situated where the play-ground was soon to be, were being relocated to vacant plots further down the site where ever possible. George and his wife were not too unhappy about being moved as the further one goes down the allotment site, the greener and more rural the area becomes.

"Yes, I am. Pleased to meet you."

"I've seen your friend down here a lot, working away. She said she was having trouble with the couch grass. All over the place she said it was."

Not to be outdone, I countered with, "Well, I think the worst problem is the bramble roots, they're so deep-rooted and tough that it takes ages to get even one out and our plot is covered with them." I leaned on my fork, feeling like a real gardener trading facts and opinions with the best of them. "Still given the state this plot was in, I don't think we've done too badly, all in all."

"Yeah, you look as though you are coming along all right." He took a drag and squinted at the carpet laid out over most of No 64. "I'm busy at the moment getting our new allotment ready. I'm moving the turf from the old site to make the paths on the new one," he threw me a glance from under his hat, "I'm only taking our own soil what belongs to us." I murmured reassuringly, every serious allotmenter was rather paranoid about being mistaken for a rip-off merchant.

"I come up here to see if 'e could help me move our shed up." He gestured in the direction of Bernie's neighbour.

"It's concrete. I made it myself at 'ome and brought the panels down here one by one on the bike. I've got my nephew coming down to help me, but I think it'll take four of us to shift it."

"Concrete," I murmured admiringly, "I bet that doesn't get broken into".

"Nah, I laid the base myself an all, but I won't be able to shift it on me own."

I am ever ready to see what other people are doing on their plots, so I asked George if I could take a look at his. We went down the path and found his two admirably laid-out sites, four foot beds separated by neat grass paths with a dramatic pink trellis arrangement at the rear of one of them and a white trellis pinned to the side of his wooden shed (which had been left by a previous tenant).

He'd obviously put in a lot of work and in a relatively short space of time. "I found this trellis in a skip", he said pointing to the white one, "and that one down there too." The pink one reminded me of one of those delicate attempts at partitioning you find in the too-naice-for-the-likes-of-you tea-shops you can still find in fading English sea-side resorts. Food emporia where the tables are too small and tight for comfort and the sandwiches likewise.

I really don't know what us allotmenters would do without skips. We recycle so much material on our plots that others have chucked away that almost nothing goes to waste. But even I was impressed with the pink trellis work.

"Where's this shed then?" I asked, curious. We went down to the area, soon to be concreted over in favour of the childrens' extra play space, and there was the shed. I remembered it as soon as I saw it. I had passed it lots of times before. It was taller than the average shed and stood out from the general tone of its surroundings on its solid concrete base, topped with a corrugated metal lid.

The general look of wooden sheds around and about the allotments tends to the slightly crest-fallen by comparison with this stout example. Shabby and leaning, with panels invariably missing and locks kicked in, the general shed variety lacked the imposing uprightness of this specimen.

Trouble was it had always reminded me of one of those mysterious electricity huts you come across in the country, usually surrounded by an iron fence and warning signs of "DANGER, LIVE ELECTRICITY. 10,000,000 VOLTS. KEEP OUT."

"Feel the weight of that door," George commanded. I moved it, a little, it weighed a ton. I poked my head inside and out again, very rapidly. There was something claustrophobic and sealed about this shed above and beyond the usual confined space.

"I reckon if you got stuck in there, you'd suffocate," said George with a strong note of pride tinged with warning in his voice, "it's completely airtight, just a touch of damp that I need to sort out when I move it."

I felt like asking whether he shouldn't put a DANGER, KEEP OUT notice on it anyway. It would be a bit hard on a vandal to end up in a life threatening situation over a pair of wellies or a spade.

*

I was rigid with excitement. A bolt of pure interest shot through me, which was highly unusual given the circumstances. I was watching the nation's favourite soap-opera.

My involvement in the plot-line has almost completely disappeared from any soap that I now watch. Thirty years of familiarity with the genre, means that I can predict a story and its outcome, weeks in advance of its final, tor-

89

tured denouement on screen and the proliferation of soaps results in themes being continually recycled from soap to soap. Like life, there is not much that's new in Soap World.

Why do I still watch them then? There's no answer to that.

Tonight though, Mavis, and her own personal Butthead, Derek, were talking about getting an allotment! They were full of the hopeful anticipation we have all felt at the prospect of their own patch of land.

Allotments had gained Street-cred. Or as much cred as Mavis and Derek can lend any venture. I wondered why this soap hadn't given someone an allotment much earlier on in its existence, like its main rival. After all, the spirit of allotmenting is culturally accepted as being a Northern phenomenon, adopted (and bastardised) by the South. What's more, this soap was packed with characters oozing allotment stereotypes and, in my opinion, Mavis and Derek were not in the van of these characters.

I would be watching developments with a heightened critical awareness.

*

We had been hoping and expecting to start planting seeds directly into a spring-warmed soil by about the end of the month, but continuing frosts made us cautious. Our soil still looked heavy, lumpy and lifeless and not the warm, welcoming blanket our seeds needed.

Instead, we had a session of sewing seeds into trays for later transplanting, round at my friend's house which, fortunately, came equipped with compost and enough space to lay out all the paraphernalia necessary for the job. To whit: trays, tray-bottoms to catch water run-off, clear-plastic tray tops to cover the eventually sewn seeds, marker sticks for indentification, pencils to write on marker sticks, water sprays to water seeds, compost and jugs to get compost from sacks and into trays.

We mostly set out rows of tomato seeds, after carefully washing and disinfecting our trays in baths of fluid strong enough to remove the skin from our hands. These lines of various varieties of tomato, one of my favourite salad crops, came in all shapes and sizes, from huge, fat red ones, long, globular Italian types, to the striped, tigerish kind and we had even fallen for the small, neat yellow cousins. Also included were basil and parsley, celeriac and celery seeds — anything that we felt needed a bit of extra T.L.C.

What with egg-boxes of chitting potatoes and trays of various germinating seeds on every window-sill and spare square of floor, very soon my flat looked like a cross between a fairly permanent nursery and a fairly temporary squat. Humans were restricted in their living and moving space in case they knocked something over. They felt unable to relax and expand and leave coffee cups and newspapers lying around in case that very space was about to be commandeered and claimed for yet another tray of seeds.

Of course I got cross-eyed looks from the partner at this invasion of the killer tomatoes, but he wisely forbore to complain, deciding to take the longer view that he would be pushing enough of the eventual produce down his neck to warrant tolerance at this juncture.

My friend dazzled me once more, by producing plans of both plots detailing where every crop was to be located and how much of each bed was to be allocated to that crop. These plans proved to be terribly useful. As we tended to visit the allotments at different times we were able to coordinate our activities via these plans without duplicating each others efforts or getting in the way of what the other person was doing.

Thus I knew where to put my Second Early potatoes in ground which had been particularly kept free of limed compost as per the plan and my friend planted up significant quantities of onion sets in the areas pre-ordained for that purpose. In fact, without these plans, I think it would have been impossible for us to have made any progress at all. I think we would have never really known at any point what went where and who had done what. The plans were a natural progression from and fulfilment of the famed crop rotation scheme which had been so arduously completed weeks earlier.

It was a marvel to me to realise that each bed on our two allotments was designated a role in the rotation cycle which then determined not only which vegetables were to be grown in it, but how that bed was to be composted and fertilised. There was order and system.

This was a novelty for two individuals who mutually confessed to very little system and order in almost every other area of their lives.

Chapter 15
April's Fools

Chinese Proverb

A hole in the ice is dangerous only to those who go skating.

My friend and I agreed to spend a morning together on the allotments so that we could catch up on progress and confer as to the priorities for the next month. In general our system of planning worked very well and even though we did not spend much time on the allotments together, there was a faint suggestion of gradual progress and little mutual disruption. We felt pleased that we were managing to work independently and yet in common.

From time to time though, we needed to meet. We found it useful to agree, face to face, when to plant out various seeds as we examined the soil and shook our heads, dubious over the continually cold weather. We would tour our range and explain odd changes to the other, that, for example, a dubious patch of wilting green was, in fact, some exciting fruit bushes, generously donated by an allotment neighbour.

At our meetings, we usually ended up in a state of excitement and euphoria. We would just enthuse each other so extravagantly and be so thrilled with our progress and so hopeful of what was to come that we would soon be slinging lavish compliments at one another, delighted that we had undertaken this venture together and not alone.

There was so much to share in the thrill of growing itself, in the satisfaction of developing our plots and in the reassurance of being able to confer with one another, that I do believe that we doubled the fun in doing it together. Had I gone ahead on my own and had an allotment all to myself, I think that the pressures of everyday life on top of those of the allotment itself, would have meant that I would have given up and retired hurt.

I felt that I had the best of all worlds.

The day was April Fool's Day, not chosen, but coming to pass for this morning of mutual endeavour, probably because the gods felt like a bit of a laugh. It was a bright, brisk day. We plonked ourselves next to the path on No 64 and started off by getting out the flasks of coffee and cold breakfast-toast, squatting on the hand-made kneeler, DIY'd in wood by my friend's husband — for all the world like ageing Brownies camping out for the first time, dodging responsibility and Tawny Owl.

We got into the gossip.

We had shifted into top gear as Joan passed us on the way down to her plot. Friendly greetings were exchanged. My friend knows Joan better than I and so introduced me. After a few moments of this allotment badinage we got on with our work.

I was weeding (yet again) the top two beds in No 64, while my friend was digging (yet again) into the never-diminishing acreage of wilderness always remaining on this very same plot.

Only a few moments later, Joan came hurrying up to us, obviously very upset. She was calling to us as she approached.

"They've burned down the sheds. Somebody's burned down the sheds," she was shocked and hurt and frightened and angry, her voice cracking as she kept on, "vandals! Vandals have burned down two sheds. Come and see. Quick."

We dropped what we were doing and hurried down the path with her, trying to calm her down, trying to soothe her. She was obviously so upset that we became upset and anxious too.

We got down to the area of wreckage. It was a Monday morning, early. All that was left of two previous sheds were two almost identical charred piles of remains which had pieces of spade, fork, rake and hoe head littered among them, the wooden handles having disappeared in the blaze.

We were quiet for a moment as we looked at the mess left over. Whoever had done this (and we all thought it was probably the children/youths who regularly plagued our allotments with petty thefts), had done so on Sunday evening, because they had been fine and standing as usual all the previous day.

A piece of exciting fun for kids; a brief, hot blaze that was probably over in half an hour. For the people who had owned the sheds, possibly for years, there was the expense of replacing all the tools, collected and cared for over those years. All the odd but useful items gathered and stored for future use that every allotmenter has tucked away — magpie booty that holds purely personal meaning and purpose, but which is often irreplaceable — had gone up in smoke.

And there was the shed itself. A gift when an allotmenter first arrives, but costing real money to replace should anything happen to it. Negative events were gradually overtaking all our sheds. Down the long central path along which our sheds stood, regular as sentries, many gaps were appearing, as they were kicked or pushed in or hacked down or burned by faceless vandals. Most people did not bother to replace them, preferring to hide their tools around the allotment or to bring them from home on each visit.

There was nothing we could do. I later reported the incident to Jacky of Allotment Leisure Services and she mourned with us, but there was little that she could do either. We were not about to be granted a permanent police presence or an eight foot, electrified fence around the total perimeter of the site. Restless youths would always be able to get in and find something to damage or steal.

Joan was so upset for the two people, friends of hers, who owned the sheds, she said that, at that moment, she didn't even want to go on with her allotment. That frankly the incident had left such an unpleasant taste, that allotmenting was permanently spoiled for her. She could not keep starting again, replacing items that were stolen or pointlessly destroyed. She left soon afterwards, her day spoiled and went to tell one of the shed owners of the rotten thing that had been done to them.

My friend and I were rather subdued afterwards. We agreed, however, some damage was inevitable and that we would just have to accept that crops would be stolen and some of our things would go missing. Overall, however, that as long as we allowed for the inevitability of these unpleasant things happening, that we would continue to enjoy our plots and would refuse to get depressed and discouraged.

That morning, as more people came to put in their first shift of the week, the talk was all of the fire. They stood around in groups repeating the same phrases to each other, commiserating and hating the fact that something so unpleasant should have happened to such a nice couple of people. We also wondered who would be the next to suffer? Who would be the next to have some serious damage done to their crops or have their property stolen? Even more menacing, was the impending threat that now one fire had been started, another was likely to happen soon.

We were a community under seige, with no defences.

*

I chose an evening a few days later, allotmenting to go. The weak sun was doing its best to give an illusion of Spring, though the wind laughed in its face and stung mine. I felt quite brave going down there, by myself after 4 pm, given that our vandal-youth generally operated at about that time and the shed burning was uppermost in my mind.

I struggled down to No 64 with my tools, work gloves and boots which I was not, of course, leaving in the shed as easy pickings and felt that in that effort alone, I had accomplished enough for one day without having to strike soil with spade, yet again, on resistant No 64.

Sulky and wavering was my mood. I plonked myself down to view the amount of work that still needed doing and to calculate how little I could get away with, commensurate with relieving my permanent guilt about not doing enough, when I saw the duck.

An ordinary brown duck, a female, according to my vast knowledge of wildlife. She was perusing the faded patch of spinach when I noticed her and then, dissatisfied, she proceeded to wander along the bed in a lost and listless attitude, very similar to my own. I watched her as she literally wandered off, not flew, south in the direction of Richmond Park and the company of other ducks and more congenial watery environments.

I think that she must have heard a rumour about the new, improved and big pond that my friend was going to dig to accommodate the desires of her frog and newt-loving son. If the unique appearance of Lady Duck was a harbinger of wildlife to come once the pond was constructed, I was all for it.

We were already providing some degree of wet-lands in the form of the bucket-size ponds which were hidden on one side of No 64 and over which I somehow managed to trip with tedious regularity. The new pond was going for growth. I was particularly pleased because if and when dug, it would occupy a large area of yet undug (and to my mind, never to be cultivated) No 64. It was to be sited between two elder flower trees and boded well to be a scenic feature, fit for picnicing and entertaining by.

I turned up at the allotments, one day some week or so

later, having been waylaid by the pressure of earning a living and was stung by the size of the hole that my friend's husband had carved into the ground. Mounds of the excavated earth stood to one side, abandoned and surplus to requirements. After this, progress was swift and soon the pond had lining and pond plants and some landscaping of stones to hide the black plastic rim — but this was not entirely complete. The landscaping also included two compost heaps, various bags of guinea-pig litter, newspapers and various items of wood. There was some further work to be done, I thought, before I would be inviting selected friends to *soirées* round the soothing water feature.

My friend's boy took to the project with delight and was happy to tell me about the number of newts collected and frog-spawn spawned. We developed a good conversational exchange, he keeping me up-to-date with new developments, me decrying frog-spawn but not frogs and agitating for some Japanese Koi carp in place of newts.

I was due to go off for a bit of R & R for two weeks and so rushed to get some of my chitting Earlies (potatoes) in before I left. This I undertook with some trepidation because, in veg. growing circles, everyone raises potatoes and getting it wrong on this vegetable equated to being bowled out for a duck.

Of course it decided to rain as I was compulsively reading my instruction book, for one final time, before getting to it, but I was not to be put off.

Six inches deep, twelve inches apart and eighteen inches separating each row. I kept repeating these distances like a mantra as I put in each potato, working to the rythmn of the words and initially nervous in case I got the spaces mixed up. I gradually relaxed. I began to judge each six inch depth and twelve inch gap by sight, keeping a fairly even row, though I had not spread out a taught string to keep my line — more fiddling about in the rain was not what I needed then.

Despite the rain it was a good moment. Potatoes are easy to plant and the feeling of satisfaction once I had them all in the ground, was warm. I spared a moment to be concerned for the future of earthing-up and exactly when and how that was to be achieved to facilitate a batch of healthy, prolific and tasty potatoes, but sufficient unto the day...

Chapter 16
May. Has it Really Been Eleven Months?

Proverb

*When you can tread on nine daisies at once,
spring has come.*

There were few other indicators. Daisies we had in plenty
along with nettles, couch grass, short stubby grass and the
long, wavy prairie variety. Everything on the allotments
was exploding up through the ground with well-being and
vitality. But we had no spring. Cold, grey and generally
not a bit like spring as we expected it.

Mac on, I went down to the allotments.

The first thing I noticed after admiring the way the
weeds had reconquered their former territory in so many
of the beds I thought I had cleared before my holiday, was
that the bag of barb-e-ques which I had carefully hidden in
the back bushes on No 64,in the wake of the shed-burning,
had gone.

Someone had obviously come across them and my old
gardening boots which I had also hidden near by. With the
promised approach of spring and summer these two, small
travelling size barb-es would come in handy. Not so the old
boots which were still there.

The BarBs would have to be replaced, because they did-
n't belong to me, they were friend Jane's and she was keen
on *al fresco* dining.

The third change I noticed was that No 64 had a new

neighbour to its right. This plot which had been Eric's had lain idle for a period after his death the previous year, though his wife and son had tried to keep things going for a while. Periodically, however, E.T.B. walked round the site, doing his "assessment". This meant that any allotment holder not pulling their weight and keeping things up to puff could have the lotty equivalent of their licence revoked and find their plot reassigned to another. Generally illness or problems at home or work meant that a period of grace was always given and plots would not be whipped away overnight, but given the demand for allotments, none could be allowed to remain uncultivated for ever.

I went over and introduced myself to my new neighbour. This was Ralph. He had apparently been gardening at home with his wife for twenty years or so, but after about ten years they had taken stock and decided that they were no good at it! This begged the obvious question, then why take on an allotment? But, I, who couldn't garden at all, had ended up taking on two of them, so, as with many of the deeper questions of life, logic just doesn't apply when it comes to allotments.

Fresh back from holiday and with an equally fresh perspective, I mentally totted up our successes and failures over the previous eleven months of allotmenting. Half of No 64 was dug and the other half sported a pond. Much still remained to be cleared, however, and the weeds seemed to come back on this plot, much quicker than on Liam's, probably because the latter had been so consistently well worked in the past. No 64, though still in the process of being wrung from virgin rain forest, had provided a good array of salad crops and runner beans last year and overall the ground was softer and easier to work than the clay base of Liam's.

We had almost finished reordering Liam's and were nearly up-to-date on what needed to be done on that plot. Everything from composting to weeding, to seed planting to transplanting, virtually everything was current.

We had had no real luck with our over-wintering, though, and we probably wouldn't try that again as it was a waste of time and money. None of the peas had survived; the kohlrabi had bolted and failed to develop. The mooli seemed to have disappeared altogether and our over-wintered onions were smaller than the sets planted in March. We did feel proud that the broad beans seemed to be doing well and our fennel that had spent the winter under a pane of glass, was tall and boasted strong yet exquisitely feathered branches, beautiful plumes of waving green.

Our potatoes were also busy coming up, so it was almost time for me to worry about the earthing-up process. We also had several spring cabbages, lamb's lettuce, leeks, spinach, kale, garlic and spring onions, so with judicious picking, we could more or less eat a freshly grown vegetable from our allotments every day.

Not bad for beginners.

*

By this time, the lotty had become a spiritual home of sorts. If not engaged in earning money or actually asleep in bed, then time spent on every other activity had to be carefully weighed against the value of that time put in on the allotments.

There is always something to do. In fact, there is always too much to do on our plots. I'm not sure if other allotmenters feel the same pressure — probably they're better organised or more proficient or don't work. We, however, had pared down our lives to cope with our two plots — so much so in fact, that for me, the question of whether or not we could continue to run two of them was still unresolved.

It might seem that I wasn't suffering too much in the effort to keep the vegetable production line going. And that's true of course. But, having been used to doing things with free time other than "go down to the allotments", I was cutting back on choices. Saturdays, for example, were almost entirely spent on getting ready to "go down to the allotment" (ie getting the gardening gear out from the washing basket where it had lain in the vain hope of being washed since its last outing; getting a flask of coffee together as well as items for lunch), being at the allotment (which generally lasted from three to four hours) and staggering home and into the bath to recover from the achingly hard work of having been on the allotment. All of this being rounded-off by falling asleep, exhausted from all the unaccustomed physical work and fresh air.

The partner began to suggest that I was becoming "obsessed" by the allotments. An idea that I hotly rejected as I reminded him that, if he was missing my company, there was an easy way to resolve the problem.

Bad weather and by that only really heavy rain, snow or below zero temperatures could be taken for granted as a reason not to visit the lotty. Every other "excuse" somehow had to be justified. Illness was just acceptable; a weekend away with friends was really not.

Where was all this pressure coming from? To whom, you might wonder, was I having to justify myself? Who or what was tweaking my guilt nerve labelled "doing my duty by the allotments"? My friend? E.T.B.? The allotment Overlords? None of these had that much power over me. No, the pressure exerted was largely coming from the lotties themselves. Now that we had begun to transform the sites and to actually grow our own food, the pressures of keeping up with the demands of each season, which were ten times as exacting in Spring as at other times, kept me at it.

Everything became personal. Having planted seeds and transplanted them as seedlings, for example, it became an internal imperative to water the things, weed them, feed them, and generally look after them, until they decided to play nice and reward me by producing some real food crops. I suppose it was the ancient nurturing instinct that kept me going. That, or more likely, sheer bloody mindedness. Whether I had the essential feel for mother nature and the rythmn of the earth that we now know that American Indians, among an enlarging band of sundry others, have in bundles or whether I was just damned if, having invested so much time and effort so far, I'd throw in the trowel now, might possibly remain one of life's quintessential mysteries.

I mused on this effect as I heaved at an enormous clump of weed-ridden sod on Liam's plot. I was starting to clear the last bed that had to be turned as part of our process of reorganisation; it was also very weedy and extremely impacted, probably because most of the bed had spent its life as a path, under Liam's ownership, and it was well trodden and solid-as-a-rock earth. I was sick of clearing ground by now. It is back-breaking work, slow and though very necessary, it is not half as much fun as everything else — except weeding. So, I had stopped for a rest, after about two spade fulls.

As I rested, panting and slightly dizzy from the effort, a robin hopped over to within eight inches of me and eyed me with interest. I have never been that close to a wild bird before, apart from park ducks and swans, whose attention is usually focused on the half ton of bread it takes to keep them happy.

Nonchalantly, the robin delicately picked up one or two worms I had exposed from the digging, but was in no real hurry to move on and it bobbed even closer to me. I was stirred by the moment. I held my breath in case I moved or disturbed this charming creature and drove it away. We watched each other; representatives from alien worlds, trying to calculate what made the other click. At that moment, I understood why there are so many wildlife programmes on TV — it is obviously far better fun for the TV makers than filming politicians, the news or even smart cookery presenters.

The tension was broken by the rain coming down in

bucketfuls and the robin pushed off, smartish, not concerned about prolonging what I felt had been a true encounter of the third kind.

I sat on the flower pot in Liam's and poured a contemplative cup of coffee. This was the spiritual, soul-singing side of allotmenting. Fortunately, my friend turned up soon after I began to think poetic thoughts, in the manner of Wordsworth, and cut short what was threatening to become a very maudlin and "personal" moment. She had not come to do any work, but to talk over a few private matters with me and at the allotment, in the rain, under a leaking roof, sitting on flower pots and drinking coffee from plastic cups, were, for us, the ideal conditions under which to share our private problems.

*

The end of this first month of official Spring was a high spot at the allotment association. E.T.B. organised an Open Day, an opportunity for allotmenters in other areas to come and visit our site, share information, opinions and to meet one other.

I arrived about 10:30am to find that the party was in full swing. More people than ever I'd seen before, swilling round the association shed as they swilled wine and munched crisps and pointed and opined on our efforts. E.T.B. had really spared no expense. There was lots to drink and enough bits and pieces to eat and he'd organised people, magically equipped with lapel badges, to act as official "meeters and greeters". It raised the atmosphere on this surprisingly bright morning of the Spring Bank Holiday and put everyone in the festive spirit.

I failed in my social duty and ducked out of sight at the back of Liam's, nervous of being asked a technical question by a visitor, which I was sure to get wrong and so let our side down. I noticed that Bernie, despite being arrayed in an official hostess badge, was also adopting the same tactic, though her plot, being a riot of colour and flowering variety, was attracting lots of attention.

The garden party finished about 12:30, probably because our allotmenting visitors were anxious to get back to their own plots and wring changes from their sites — fuelled by the example of what we had managed to achieve, not to mention being fuelled by all the free booze. I was still head down on a particularly tricky section of transplanting at about 1:30pm when a co-hort called out to me as he hustled off down the path, "It's lunch time. You're allowed to take a break now you know. I am, I'm off down the pub."

Not for me. I had exactly thirty five small tomato plants to find room for. Not only room, but each plant had to have its supporting stick, which meant that I spent ages wandering around the whole area picking up and discarding bits of wood, or abandoned and broken cane, even metal stakes I dragooned into service. Each tomato was then carefully tied to its companion stick and given a generous dowsing of water, once finally settled in its own hole. I got splinters, cuts and nicks, but I got those tomatoes in the ground and then went home and died.

Chapter 17
June. But More, Much More Than This...
I Did It My Way.

Turkish Proverb
*Experience is a precious gift, only given a man
when his hair is gone.*

Suddenly, down on the plots, there was more work to do
than you could shake a stick at. From grey, freezing temperatures and a zero Spring, June fell on us with hot,
sunny weather and crops insisting that they be tended.

Fortunately, my friend responded to the demands of
nature's busiest season with manic intensity and kept the
tide of work at bay. I limped along behind, transplanting a
bit here and sowing a bit there and adding the occasional
session with the hose for good measure.

I noticed that we tended to have smaller amounts of
more veg. than the average plot. A casual glance around
the whole area laid open the fact that many lotty-people
seemed to want to eat only potatoes and onions with a few
tomatoes and other salad crops thrown into the remaining
spaces. Often as much as a half a plot would be given over
to potatoes and onions featured prominently among the
rest. Other veg. fought for their rights in the remnant of
cultivatable space.

Several of our beds, however, were divided in half or
thirds with different crops from the same family. We had
created a patchwork effect of growing space with different

crops at different stages of development, some covered with fleece, some with green netting and the odd wig-wam of poles here and there for our various beans.

We had early carrots sharing a bed with onions and leeks; tomato plants hustled for space along with the outriders of our strawberry plants and in one bed alone, spring onions sat with garlic, corn salad, spring greens and first potatoes — an allotment tenement bordering on the slum dwelling.

This state of affairs was understandable given how overboard we had gone with the seed catalogues. We had ordered some of nearly everything, wanting diversity and variety in what we grew and, more importantly, in what we eventually ate. We were also curious as to whether or not we would be able to grow most of these crops, so there was some rational of trial and error behind this medley. But, the real reason for the variety was that, faced with the seed catalogues, we reverted to type and immediately wanted it all, there was no way we were going to exercise judicial and selective choice — home shopping meets the allotment.

One pays a price for one's pleasures as we all know and, in this case, the price was not mere pounds and pence, but in extra effort on the allotments. Splendid diversity means lots of extra work. The potato people had it easy once the spuds were in; they sat back, with their tea and sandwiches and watched the vigourous plants spread and grow. There was no thinning, transplanting nor much weeding, as potatoes spread over the ground, so you cannot see if there is any trouble developing underneath.

For us, though, the first couple of very warm weeks in June meant that we were running around trying to get all the various seeds in, before their due sowing time was up. Simultaneously, salad crops had to be thinned, young cabbage and brussels planted out; courgettes "got in"; carrots down (with the accompanying construction of a carrot-fly barrier, which, as it consisted of glass panels, blew over in the wind, scattering glass in paths and beds alike and giving me a nice alternative occupation, in case I was growing bored). Peas did not lay themselves out with accompanying pea-sticks and/or supportive netting — one did that for them. Beans, likewise, though clamouring for tall, bamboo supports did not just get on and bring them with them — one muggins or another had to see to it and remembering all the old lessons from Blue Peter, get busy with string, scissors and bamboo poles.

Meanwhile, somewhere had to be found for the spinach, assorted cabbages, broccoli permanent and the every day broccoli-broccoli, the Swiss chard, cucumber, celeriac and celery. It all found a home. I generally did not remember where these homes were, five minutes after they moved in — but by the middle of June, I was beyond caring, I was just pleased that the activity level seemed to be easing off a little. By the middle of June, also, there was the dawn of that period of delight which I remembered so vividly from last year, food began to take shape and look like food and there was stuff that could be picked and eaten.

As the salad crops were thinned, and they, precious green salad veg. that they are, were no sooner seeds than they were small lettuces, rocket, and radishes. They grew at an astonishing rate and the thinnings could be eaten. I gorged on salad, young, sweet and a tender green. My friend gorged on radishes, hot, peppery and seemingly everlasting. We both picked young spinach and half expected that the miracle of new growth would stop working and that we would permanently damage the plants. But, tougher than the Gladiators, the spinach would grow right back at us, providing almost inexhaustible supplies.

The warmer weather brought with it more people out and about on their allotments, though the peak times were limited to the early morning and evening when the heat lifted a little to allow work and watering. The rest of the time the allotment site simmered in its own heat-haze, virtually deserted or dotted with the exceptional group or two who had managed to arrange their own shade and sustenance, some equipped with all the comforts of their patios

109

— deck chairs, tables, BBQs and drinks.

We had decided to abandon the hope of continuing to turn over No 64, this year. Though a good third of it remained uncleared or uncovered by pond, we were too stretched in keeping on top of all the other veg. activity to try and dig through healthy weed and grass cover, baked ground and carpet — especially in the heat-wave. Even the carpet was looking decidedly worn and ragged under the strain of trying to keep our unusually vigourous weed-life at bay. In many areas it had forsaken the unequal struggle. I knew that I could relax when my friend, usually eternally optimistic about what we could achieve, admitted that this area was probably not going to get done this year.

The elder trees, one in front and one behind the pond, had blossomed and provided an attractive area of shaded greenery round the not-yet-attractive-but-bursting-with-potential-pond. We congregated one balmy Saturday morning to have our break before the work began, only slightly inconvenienced by the strong sewage smell which emanated, not from the pond you might be thinking, but from the bucket of organic fertiliser that my friend had concocted from soaking nettles in water. Though covered by a two-inch thick piece of wood, the power of this organic brew was strong, engendering in me much faith that it would be equally forceful on the tomato plants — its eventual destination.

Things were looking good and we were proud. My friend could rightly be particularly proud of her achievements, as she bore the brunt of the work; my work (for money) becoming almost full-time.

We chatted about the future landscaping of our wild water garden (which we had drifted into calling the pond area) and rubbed suntan cream into our fair English skins, to ward off the red, weather-beaten look of the Flower Pot Men.

I was particularly conscious of the ageing effects of so much outdoor work, regularly rubbing Factor 25 into all exposed parts, of which there were probably too many.

Short shorts, skimpy t-shirts, and sunglasses topped with a truly awful straw hat, were my normal mode in hot weather — gear that I frankly would not have been buried in, but somehow I assumed masses of carefree licence once on the allotment.

I felt that I had been somewhat encouraged in this look by Desmond, who, while thrusting four spring onions (which turned out to be garlic) into my hand one Sunday afternoon, ordered, "Have these," in an interestingly foreign accent, "you have nice legs." More male praise than I'd been on the receiving end of in fifteen years — no wonder it had gone to my head.

A major disappointment of this period was the disappearance of the strawberries. Fruit was fairly vulnerable on the allotments, much more so than vegetables. Gooseberries had been taken from one woman's plot already this year throwing her into anger and upset and sensible fruit growers generally constructed some form of fruit cage to present, at least a token barrier, to potential fruit-nappers.

By the last week in June, we had not one strawberry left on our runners, when only the week before I had carefully laid straw nests around and under our crop of green and ripening fruit, wondering at my own diligence. At that time there had been about five ripe strawbs and my friend and I had eaten them up, delightedly — anticipating our crop.

A week later when we met, my friend asked, cautiously, "Did you have any strawberries?"

"Yes, I had about two. Why?" Terrier-like I was instantly alerted to the fact that there was "A Problem".

"Well, there are none left now. The pigeons must have had them." My friend had obviously been wondering if I had loaded-up with the fruit and left none for her, which would have been a first, as we were normally scrupulous in only taking our fair shares.

"What, not one left? Not even any green ones? There were loads there last week." My voice rising an octave with each question.

"Well, there are none there now," replied my friend who was being Mature, while I was being Frustrated. "The birds must have got at them. We must remember to net them up next year. Which reminds me, we'll probably need to get some more green netting soon, we're running out..."

To be honest, I'd stopped listening. I was peeved about the strawberries. The few that I'd had, had tasted wonderful, like so much else that we grew, chemical-free, own food was quite different from the shop-bought variety. And I'd spent a fruitless (sic) hour mulching-up our young fruit to keep it out of the jaws of slugs and to prevent it from rotting on the ground, when I should have spent the time protecting it from the menace from above, The Birds.

Still, as always, there was too much else to be getting on with to be able to pout and mutter for long. I went instead to put in another row of peas, followed by a touch of judicious hoeing with our new, "real" hoe. This had proved to be an absolute miracle-worker. A hoe with a flexible rather than a fixed head, it cuts through weeds, effortlessly, and even recommends that you leave the weeds on the surface to rot, rather than picking them all up afterwards.

This reduces the boring and back-breaking time spend hoeing, by about two thirds and, unsurprisingly, I've become keen on hoeing, since it's become so easy to do. I am a lazy gardener, as you've probably gathered and will adopt any short cut to get a job done, which results in the least inconvenience to myself. In life, so as in the garden.

*

I still don't think that I've got the right attitude to gardening even after one whole year of owning a half share in two allotments. I think the majority of my allotment colleagues view me with good will, but mildly askance, as if not quite knowing how to place me — a bit like a vegetable, of dubious flavour, that is likely to bolt and run to seed before producing anything of real, solid value.

Still, the fraternity is highly tolerant and we rub along. I'm looking forward to the next twelve months. I've got a long way to go before I reach the median 15 — 20 years that some of these people have invested in owning their allotments. And who knows what I might try next, what new, exotic veg. I might want to experiment with? Or, perhaps I'll boldly go completely allotment-mad and try growing prize leeks or cabbages and become immersed in the arcane world of the produce show.

There may be no end to all this.

The Epilogue

Proverb
Those that are afraid of wounds, must not come nigh a battle.

Looking back over my progress over the course of twelve months, I am definitely pleased; tired, but pleased. From owning a rather small balcony to half of two allotments, even if one of those is rather more carpet and pond than allotment, feels like an achievement.

I continue to be delighted and amazed every time we produce some vegetable or other that is edible. I find it hard to come to terms with the fact that this is how all vegetables start life, as seeds in the soil and are not merely found in supermarkets, wrapped in plastic. I think the food does taste better, picked straight from our chemical-free allotment and it certainly does not last as long as shop-bought. Lettuces picked one day and left in the fridge are wilting and limp the following day.

There is a lot of work associated with allotment ownership and I don't think I could seriously contemplate owning even one allotment on my own. I am intensely fortunate in the good will and hard work of my friend and when we do meet together on the site, then the very sharing of the work feels good and better than the lone effort.

I am at a disadvantage in keeping fully up-to-date with the varied seasonal demands of our allotments because I have a job. I don't wish to discourage people who have full-time employment from owning one, however, because there are people who manage to work, have a family and run an allotment, all very successfully. I am not one of them, more's the pity. I have a definite energy deficiency.

But allotment-sharing is a good idea for people who want to come together to share the work and the expense and the eventual goodies. This arrangement enhances the social nature of allotment ownership and helps your site to "become a more active community" as E.T.B. recently wrote to me.

In short, I'm a fan.

I am viewed as slightly cracked in certain circles, where the allotment is still viewed as being a relic of wartime Britain and fit only for the aged and the somewhat dull. Thank heavens, otherwise these rather well-kept secrets would be over-run by the trendies and would lose so much of their charm.

As to whether or not we will keep owning two allotments, or let one go due to the pressure of competing responsibilities, I think the jury is still out. If my friend is happy to undertake the bulk of the burden and let me do what I can, when I can, then I would be eager to keep them both. If not, it would be hard to have to decide which one to let go — they each have their pros and cons.

For the time being things will go on as they are, the cycle continuing into another year.

My allotment colleagues also seem to have decided that I am here for the duration, as I recently received a letter from E.T.B., that though owning an allotment, I was not a member of the Barnes Horticultural & Allotments Society — which is true, I'm not. I have something of an antipathy to "joining" things and generally, do not behave well once joined — I slope off and am rarely seen again.

I will join this association, however, an indication of how strongly I feel about the allotments and, as the letter appealed to my better nature by asking, "Please help us and all your neighbours by belonging... looking forward to better relationships all round." Absolutely, me too.

Postscript

My friend submitted our big pumpkin in the September produce show — and we won *first* prize!

Our first pumpkin effort was judged superior to the competition (ie. 3 other pumpkins) and we won a certificate and £1.00 (80p really after paying the 20p entrance fee).

Proud?! The word doesn't come close to describing how we feel.

ALSO AVAILABLE FROM FIVE LEAVES

The Allotment: Its Landscape and Culture
David Crouch and Colin Ward

A new edition of this classic book on allotment life, history and culture. **The Allotment** includes everything you need to know about allotments apart from horticulture. **The Allotment** has spawned no less than four television programmes, the last being **The Plot** on Channel 4. This new edition updates the struggle to hold onto allotment land and details the latest research on allotment use.

...to all of you, I recommend that classic, The Allotment
(The Observer)

Learned and literary, Crouch and Ward are like Orwellian socialists in their defence of small, important rights
(The Guardian)

David Crouch is Professor of Cultural Geography at Anglia University and the author of many articles in academic journals. Colin Ward has written numerous books on the environment, planning and housing.

326 pages : 0 907123 91 0 : £10.99

Postfree from Five Leaves, PO Box 81, Nottingham NG5 4ER.

PRESS COMMENTS ON THE ALLOTMENT

"...a wise and stimulating book, that illuminates issues way beyond the boundaries of the vegetable plot. It exposes the remoteness of many of our views about landscape. It confirms the intensity of that bond with the soil that is even now producing a new 'urban peasantry' in active revolt against mass-produced food. Its most timely contribution though, may be as a political and economic case history, of successful production that has nothing to do with the market-place, of individual enterprise that has nothing to do with greed..."

RICHARD MABEY in Sunday Telegraph

"One of the strengths of the book is the use made of oral history, as well as the authors' own acute observations and conversations with allotment holders. The special element of reciprocity which every gardener knows, the gift of spare seed, the sharing of an extra large crop, the mutual support of neighbours, is at its peak on the allotment"

GILLIAN DARLEY in Financial Times

"Every local authority planner involved with allotments should read this fascinating book. The rest of us should read it too for its meticulously researched yet highly readable insight, not only into how allotments have developed, but into their importance in the social lives of, at present, over 650,000 plot holders and their families.

GRAHAM RICE in Landscape

"The current redundancy of agricultural land suggests that the soil itself is now going the same way that the poeple went two centuries ago. The Government sees the late outcome of the Enclosures as an opportunity to adjust the farmer's slush-fund around environmental considerations and to build more executive housing. The National Trust should be equally decisive. Its officers should read this extraordinary book and then consider returning some of their redundant agricultural acres to the swelling ranks of the Digger."

PATRICK WRIGHT in The Observer

"Crouch and Ward's study covers no narrow or casual pasttime, but a popular way of life whose roots go deep into the unconscious social history of the nation... All this the authors convey... But the case which they make for the historic dignity and continued popularity of the movement should help to reverse the neglect of the past twenty years, and to safeguard the innocent, satisfying and varied pleasure which allotments can give..."

ANDREW SAINT in Times Literary Supplement